VIKING & NORSE LEGENDS FOR KIDS:

GODS, WARRIORS, MYTHS, HEROES & MORE FROM THE ANCIENT NORSE WORLD

History Brought Alive

FREE BONUS FROM HBA: EBOOK BUNDLE

Greetings!

First, thank you for reading our books.

Now, we invite you to join our VIP list. As a welcome gift we offer the History & Mythology eBook Bundle below for free. Plus, you can be the first to receive new books and exclusives! Remember it's 100% free to join.

Simply click the link below to join.

TABLE OF CONTENTS

———— ✦◇◇◉◇◇✦ ————

INTRODUCTION: WELCOME TO THE WORLD OF VIKINGS!

Close your eyes and imagine a time long ago—when the world was filled with mysterious forests, icy seas, and vast open skies. Imagine a faraway place in the North, where the winters were long and cold, a place where a people called the Vikings lived over a thousand years ago.

So, who were these Vikings? Well, they were adventurers that came from a region called Scandinavia, which is made up of three countries; Norway, Sweden, and Denmark. The vikings were known for their impressive ships that could glide across the waves like sea serpents, which they used to sail far and wide while searching for new lands, treasures, and excitement. Some Vikings were fierce warriors, wearing helmets (though not with horns—those are just props in the movies!) and carrying shields and swords. They were as brave as they were bold, always ready to explore the unknown.

But, not all that the Vikings did involved just battles and treasure; they were also farmers, traders, and storytellers. As such, they planted crops, raised animals, and traded goods such as furs, jewelry, and tools. Even when they weren't sailing the seas or working on their farms, they loved to gather around the fire and tell stories about gods and heroes, powerful beasts, and the great adventures of their ancestors.

What Is Norse Mythology?

On those chilly nights huddled around the fire, the Vikings told *myths*, which are stories full of gods, giants, and magical creatures! We call the collection of these types of stories "mythology," and many ancient societies believed in myths and stories that were unique to their culture. We call the Vikings' collection of beliefs and the stories "Norse mythology." Think of Norse mythology like a big, magical storybook, filled with tales about how the world came to be, why thunder rumbles in the sky, and even what happens when a rainbow appears.

In Norse mythology, there are mighty gods like Odin, the wise king of all gods, who wears a hat and carries a spear. He's often seen with two ravens, Huginn and Muninn, who fly across the world and tell him everything they see. Then there's Thor, Odin's son, with his magical hammer called

Mjolnir. Thor's hammer is so powerful that it can smash mountains and create thunder when he swings it! And let's not forget Loki, the trickster, who loves playing pranks on everyone—even the other gods!

The Vikings believed that the world was made up of nine *realms* (aka different worlds and lands), each of which was a place where different beings (such as the humans and the gods) lived. All realms were connected by a giant tree called Yggdrasil (try saying that three times fast!). Some examples include: Asgard, where the gods lived; Midgard, where humans like you and me live; and Jotunheim, where the giants roamed. The Vikings believed that each realm had its own unique creatures and adventures that happened in it, and together, they made up the Viking universe.

Why Do These Stories Matter?

You might wonder, "Why should I care about stories from so long ago?" Well, even ancient stories still have a lot to teach us today. The Vikings used these myths to understand the world around them—such as why lightning strikes or why the seasons change. While we now have science to explain these things, the stories of the gods and their adventures are still lots of fun and full of imagination.

However, Norse mythology isn't just about understanding nature; it's also about learning important lessons. For example, these stories can show us that we should be brave and face challenges, just like the hero Sigurd did when he fought a fierce dragon. They teach us about the importance of friendship and loyalty, like when Thor and his friends worked together to outsmart the giants. And sometimes, they remind us that playing too many tricks (like Loki) can get you into trouble!

Reading these stories will make you feel like you're there with the Vikings—sailing across the icy seas, exploring strange lands, and meeting gods and monsters. And who knows? Maybe these tales will inspire you to be brave, clever, and kind, just like the Viking heroes!

How to Use This Book

You should use this book as your very own adventure guide into the world of Vikings and the world of Norse Mythology! Inside, you'll find stories about gods, brave warriors, and magical creatures. But, don't worry, you won't need a Viking ship or a magic hammer to enjoy these tales—just a cozy spot to sit in and a big imagination!

Here's how you can get the most out of this book:

- **Start at the Beginning or Jump Around**: You can read the chapters in order, starting with the Viking gods and their world, or skip to the stories you're most curious about. If you want to know all about Thor and his hammer, jump straight to the chapter "The Epic Adventures of Thor and Loki!" Or maybe you're fascinated by mysterious creatures, in which case you should head to the chapter about trolls, dwarves, and the mighty Fenrir the wolf.

- **Look Out for Fun Facts!**: Throughout the book, you'll find special "Did You Know?"

boxes with cool facts about Viking life, like what they ate for dinner or how they built their famous longships. These will help you become a Viking expert in no time.

- **Try the Activities**: At the end of some chapters, you'll find fun activities that let you dive even deeper into the world of Norse mythology. You might get to draw your favorite Viking god, design your own magical hammer, or even write your own Viking adventure story!

- **Share the Stories**: Vikings loved telling stories, and now you can too! Share your favorite tales from the book with your family and friends, then see which god or hero they like best. Maybe you'll even create your own saga to tell around a campfire, just like the Vikings did!

- **Learn and Have Fun**: Remember, this book is all about having fun while learning something new. It's not a test, and there's no wrong way to read it. Just enjoy the stories, laugh at the silly tricks Loki pulls, cheer for the heroes, and imagine yourself becoming part of the Viking world.

Now that you know a bit more about the Vikings, Norse mythology, and the importance of these stories, it's time to begin your journey! So grab your imaginary helmet (no horns required!), and let's sail into the wonderful world of Viking legends together. Ready, set, and as the Vikings would have once said, *skål* ("cheers" in Viking language)!

CHAPTER 1:
THE VIKING GODS OF ASGARD

In this first chapter, we offer you a warm welcome to Asgard, the magical land high above the clouds where the Viking gods live! The Vikings imagined that Asgard was like a grand palace, filled with golden halls, sparkling rivers, and majestic mountains. It was a place where brave gods and goddesses gathered to protect the world and keep order in the universe. Today, we're going to meet some of the most famous and powerful gods of Asgard. So, let's take a majestic ship back in time and get ready to enter the realm of the Viking gods!

Meet Odin: The Allfather and God of Wisdom

We will first meet Odin, who is considered to be the mightiest of all the Viking gods. He's known as the *Allfather* because he's both the ruler of Asgard and the father of many gods. Odin is a bit like a king, but instead of wearing a crown, he wears a tall hat and a cloak that flutters in the wind. He's often seen with his magical spear called *Gungnir*, which never misses its target.

Odin is not just powerful; he's super wise, too! He loves to learn and is always searching for knowledge. He once gave up one of his eyes at a magical well called "Mimir's Well," just so he could gain more wisdom (meaning that he became much, much smarter than the average person). Because of that decision, he now only has one eye that shines with a deep, mysterious glow. But don't worry—Odin's sacrifice was worth it because the wisdom he gained allows him to see into the past, present, and future!

By his side, Odin has two special helpers—ravens named Huginn (Thought) and Muninn (Memory).

Every day, these clever birds fly across the world. As they fly, they gather secrets and stories, and then they return to whisper what they've learned into Odin's ear. With their help, Odin knows everything that happens in the realm of humans and beyond.

Odin is also the god of poetry and war. The Vikings believed that he would help them win battles if they honored him before going to war. Despite this brave and fierce side of him, however, the Vikings also believed that Odin had a love for the arts. As such, he was also the one who inspired the skalds (Viking poets) to write beautiful poems about heroes and gods. That's why he's as much a warrior as he is a storyteller—all rolled into one!

Thor, the Thunderer: Protector of Midgard

Next, let's meet Thor, Odin's mighty son. Thor is known as the God of Thunder, and he's as strong as a hundred warriors! He has long red hair and a beard, and is always ready for action. The Vikings imagined him as the bravest and toughest of all the gods. He was their hero, always protecting Midgard (that's the world or "realm" where humans live) from all sorts of dangers.

Thor has a powerful hammer called *Mjolnir* (pronounced MEE-ol-neer). But don't be fooled, Mjolnir is no ordinary hammer—rather, when Thor swings it, it creates lightning and makes thunder boom across the sky! The Vikings believed that every time they heard thunder, it was because Thor was up in the clouds, battling giants or evil creatures to keep Midgard safe. It is also impossible for Thor to lose Mjolnir. Even if he throws his mighty hammer far away, Mjolnir magically flies back to his hand, just like a boomerang!

Thor's favorite job is smashing giants. He especially likes to visit *Jotunheim*, the realm of the giants, to keep them in check. To get to Jotunheim or any other place he wants to go, he rides across the sky in a chariot pulled by two magical goats named *Tanngrisnir* and *Tanngnjóstr*. These goats are special because after a long journey, Thor can cook them for dinner! As long as Thor saves their bones, they will come back to life the next morning. How cool is that?

But Thor isn't just a tough warrior; he also has a big heart. He cares deeply about humans and always does his best to protect us from danger. This meant that the Vikings looked up to Thor as a symbol of bravery and strength, and they often called on him for protection during storms or before going into battle.

Loki: The Trickster with a Hidden Agenda

Now, let's talk about Loki. Loki is a bit different from the other gods because he's a trickster, which means he loves to play pranks and cause trouble. Sometimes, his tricks are funny, but other times they can get him—and everyone else—into a lot of trouble! Loki is always full of surprises, so you can never be sure if he's helping the gods or working against them.

Loki is very clever. And, to make matters more confusing, he can also change his shape to become almost anything—like a fish, a bird, or even another person! This makes him really good at sneaking around and getting out of sticky situations. But sometimes, Loki's tricks go too far, and the other gods get really mad at him.

For example, one time Loki tricked Thor into losing his hammer, Mjolnir, to a giant! Without his hammer, Thor couldn't protect Asgard or Midgard. This lack of protection made Loki realize that he had to fix the mess he created, so he came up with a plan to help Thor get the hammer back. Even though Loki can be sneaky, deep down he *almost* always knows when it's time to do the right thing.

But, Loki's history doesn't just include small and/or harmless tricks and jokes; he has a darker side too.

He's the father of some very dangerous creatures, like *Fenrir*, the giant wolf who is destined to cause trouble for the gods, and *Jormungandr*, the enormous serpent that wraps around the world. In the end, Loki's trickery will play a big role in *Ragnarok*, which is what the Vikings believed will be the great battle that brings about the end of the world. But for now, he's a mischievous, unpredictable character who keeps life in Asgard exciting!

Freya and Frey: Gods of Love, War, and Nature

Next up, let's meet Freya and Frey! The twin brother and sister who bring a little bit of magic and beauty to the world of the Vikings.

Freya is the goddess of love, beauty, and war. She's as fierce as she is beautiful, and she rides across the sky in a chariot pulled by two giant cats. Freya has a special necklace called *Brísingamen* that shines like the stars, and she's known for her magical powers. She can even travel between worlds in a cloak made of falcon feathers!

Freya is also the leader of the *Valkyries*, warrior maidens who ride into battle and choose which warriors get to go to Valhalla, Odin's great hall, after they die in battle. Valhalla is a place where brave warriors can feast and fight all day long, waiting for the final battle of Ragnarok. Freya also has her own hall called *Folkvangr*, where she welcomes other fallen warriors. She has a kind heart, but she's not afraid to stand up and fight when needed.

Her brother, **Frey**, is the god of fertility, sunshine, and nature. The Vikings believed that Frey helps plants grow, animals thrive, and the sun to shine brightly. He brings peace and prosperity, making sure that the fields are full of crops and that there's always plenty to eat. Frey rides a magical golden boar named *Gullinbursti*, whose glowing bristles light up the dark.

Frey is also known for his magical ship, *Skidbladnir*, which can not only carry all the gods but also fold up small enough to fit in a pocket! How amazing is that? Frey's power is so great that even the giants respect him, so he's always looking for ways to bring peace between Asgard and Jotunheim.

Freya and Frey are special because they belong to a different group of gods called the *Vanir*, who are known for their connection to nature and magic. But when the Vanir made peace with the *Aesir* (the group of gods pertaining to Odin), Freya and Frey came to live in Asgard, bringing a bit of their natural magic with them.

Balder: The Shining God of Light and Joy

Now let's take a look at Balder (pronounced BAL-der), who is known as the god of light, joy, and beauty. He is the son of Odin and Frigg, and everyone in Asgard loves him. Balder is a favorite amongst the gods because is kind, fair, and brings happiness with him wherever he goes. Balder is so radiant that he seems to shine like the sun. His smile can cheer up even the grumpiest giant!

Though Balder is so happy and full of sunshine, his story is surprisingly one of the saddest. One day, he began having terrible dreams that something bad would happen to him. So his mother, Frigg, asked everything in the world—plants, animals, rocks, and even water—not to harm him. Because of this, the gods would play games by throwing things at

Balder, knowing that nothing could hurt him. But there was one thing Frigg forgot to ask not to harm him—the mistletoe plant.

Loki, who we already know is always looking for mischief, tricked Balder's blind brother, *Hodr*, into throwing a spear made of mistletoe at Balder. When the spear struck him, Balder fell, and the entire world wept for his loss. The gods tried to bring him back from the underworld, but Loki's tricks prevented it.

Balder's story teaches us that though even the brightest lights can be taken away, there is hope in new beginnings, as it is prophesied (meaning "predicted") that he will return after Ragnarok.

Frigg: The Queen of Asgard and Goddess of Family

Next we'll meet Frigg (pronounced FRIG), who isOdin's wife and the queen of Asgard. She is the goddess of marriage, motherhood, and family, so naturally, she cares deeply for all her children, both godly and human. Frigg is known for her wisdom and her ability to see the future, though she never reveals what she knows.

At *Fensalir*, a beautiful hall in Asgard, Frigg weaves clouds into the sky using her magical spinning wheel. But beyond her artistic side, Frigg is also a protector of families and mothers, meaning the Vikings would ask for her blessings to keep their loved ones safe. As such a powerful matriarch (or female leader of the family), legend recounts her deep love for her son Balder, and the period of profound mourning (a word we use to describe sadness over someone's death) she went into when he died.

Frigg teaches us about the strength and love that come from family, and how important it is to care for those around us. It's true that even though she faced great sadness, she continues to be a source of comfort and strength for the gods.

Tyr: The One-Handed God of Justice

Our next acquaintance is Tyr (pronounced TEER), the god of war and justice. He is one of the bravest gods in Asgard and is always willing to do what is right, no matter how difficult it is. Tyr is famous for his role in binding Fenrir, the giant wolf who threatened the gods. To trick Fenrir into letting the gods tie him up with the magical ribbon *Gleipnir*, Tyr placed his hand in the wolf's mouth as a sign of trust.

When Fenrir realized he couldn't break free from the ribbon, he bit off Tyr's hand. From that day on, though Tyr had only one hand, he never regretted his sacrifice he had made because he knew it was for the greater good. Tyr's bravery and sense of justice made him a hero among the gods, and he has become a symbol of honor and sacrifice.

The Vikings admired Tyr for his courage and sense of duty. And just as the Vikings did, we should appreciate Tyr's story as it teaches us that doing the right thing often requires bravery, even when it means making a difficult sacrifice.

Hel: Guardian of the Underworld

Hel (pronounced HEL) is the daughter of Loki and the ruler of the underworld, called Helheim by the Vikings. Helheim is where the souls of those who didn't die in battle go to rest. Hel's realm is cold and shadowy, but she makes sure that those who enter are taken care of. Hel herself is said to be half beautiful woman and half skeleton, which represents her role as a guardian of both life and death.

Hel is not evil, but she is serious and strict, making sure that the souls in her realm stay in their place. The Vikings believed that she had the power to keep the dead from returning to the world of the living. And, though she does not live in Asgard, the gods respect her as the guardian of those who pass away peacefully.

Hel's story teaches us about both the balance between life and death and the importance of respecting the world's natural order. Her realm, Helheim, is as much a somber place as it is one of rest for those who have completed their journey in the world. This realm is the next step after life, and Hel plays an important role.

Idun: Keeper of the Apples of Youth

Idun (pronounced EE-dun) is the goddess who guards the "apples of immortality," which are what keep the gods young and strong. Without Idun's apples, the gods would not only age but also lose their powers; so, she is very important to the balance of life in Asgard.

Idun is gentle and kind, and she always carries a basket of her magical apples. However, in one legend, Loki tricked her into leaving Asgard, where she was captured by a giant. Without Idun and her apples, the gods began to grow old and weak. Loki knew he had to fix his mistake. So, he turned into a falcon, flew to the giant's home, and rescued Idun. With her return, the gods regained their youth and strength.

Idun reminds us that even the smallest and gentlest among us can have a big role to play in the world.

Her apples remind us of the importance of renewal and staying healthy!

After taking this journey through Asgard together, you can see that the gods of Asgard are as different as night and day—each with their own unique powers, personalities, and adventures. Odin is wise and mysterious, Thor is strong and fearless, Loki is tricky and unpredictable, and Freya and Frey bring beauty and nature to life. Together, they make Asgard a place of wonder and excitement.

Now that you've met the gods, you're ready to dive into their epic adventures and learn about the challenges they faced and the heroes they inspired. So, let's sail on together to the land of the Vikings, where gods and giants clash, and magical tales come to life!

Did You Know?

- The Vikings believed that a rainbow was actually a bridge called *Bifrost* that connected Asgard to Midgard (realm of the humans)!

- Thor's hammer, Mjolnir, was so heavy that not only was he the only one who could lift it, but he also needed a special pair of iron gloves to use it properly.

- Loki's children include some of the most dangerous characters in Norse mythology, like Fenrir the wolf and Hel, the goddess of the underworld.

CHAPTER 2: THE NINE WORLDS OF NORSE MYTHOLOGY

Welcome, brave adventurer, to a journey through the *Nine Worlds* of Norse mythology! Let's watch from the bow of our Viking longship as we pass a great big tree—so enormous that its branches stretch into the sky and its roots dive deep into the earth. This magical tree is called *Yggdrasil* (say it like this: IG-druh-sil), and it connects all the different realms and worlds where gods, giants, elves, and other magical beings live. Today, we're going to explore these nine incredible worlds and learn what makes each one special. So put on your Viking helmet and brace yourself as we sail into the wonders of Norse mythology!

Yggdrasil: The Great Tree That Connects Everything

Before we visit the nine worlds, let's learn about *Yggdrasil*, the giant tree that holds everything together. The Vikings believed that Yggdrasil was like a magical bridge connecting all the realms. And as what the Vikings considered to be the tree of life, it is Yggdrasil that holds the universe together with its roots and branches.

Yggdrasil's roots reach down into deep, mysterious places, like the realm of the dead, Helheim, and the well of *Mimir*, where Odin sacrificed his eye for wisdom. It even touches the icy depths of *Niflheim* and the fiery lands of *Muspelheim*. These roots are ancient and powerful, and they hold the secrets of the past, the present, and the future. Some say that those who listen closely near Yggdrasil's roots can hear the whispers of the well Mimir, which shares the ancient knowledge of the universe.

Up high in the tree's branches, the realms of the gods and other beings sway in the breeze. *Asgard*, the home of the Aesir gods, is nestled among Yggdrasil's upper branches, where Odin keeps watch over the worlds. *Alfheim*, the realm of the elves, glows with a magical light, and *Vanaheim*, the home of the Vanir gods, is full of lush greenery and peaceful valleys. Yggdrasil's branches are so strong that they hold entire worlds, cradling them like a mother protecting her children.

But Yggdrasil isn't just home to the gods; many magical creatures live within its mighty trunk. At the very top of Yggdrasil sits a mighty eagle who sees everything that is happening across the nine worlds.

The eagle's sharp gaze keeps watch over the balance between the realms, making sure that nothing slides out of place. Sitting between the eagle's eyes is a hawk named *Vedrfolnir* (VEH-dur-FOHL-neer), who may soar high above and is always on the lookout.

Down near Yggdrasil's roots lives *Nidhogg* (NID-hog), a sneaky dragon who loves to nibble at the roots. Nidhogg is always trying to weaken the tree by chewing on its roots, hoping to cause trouble between the worlds. He represents the forces of chaos that threaten to bring imbalance to the universe. But don't worry—Yggdrasil is strong and can endure the dragon's bites, just like it weathers the storms that shake its branches.

One of Yggdrasil's most mischievous inhabitants is *Ratatoskr* (rah-TAH-toss-kur), a cheeky squirrel who scurries up and down the trunk. Ratatoskr is a bit of a troublemaker because he loves to carry gossip and insults between the eagle at the top of the tree and Nidhogg down below. If the eagle says something harsh about the dragon, you can bet that Ratatoskr will run straight down to Nidhogg and make sure he hears about it. And when Nidhogg mutters back, Ratatoskr races up to spread the word to the eagle. It's like a never-ending game of telephone, meaning that there is never a dull moment between the mighty creatures of Yggdrasil.

But that's not all! Yggdrasil is also home to four stags who roam around its branches and nibble on its leaves. Their names are *Dain, Dvalin, Duneyr,* and *Durathror,* and they represent the changing seasons and the cycles of nature. As they graze on Yggdrasil's branches, they serve as a reminder that life is a cycle—just as how winter turns to spring and summer fades into autumn. They help Yggdrasil stay balanced, making sure the tree grows strong and healthy.

Yggdrasil is like the biggest and most magical treehouse you can imagine—except this treehouse holds entire worlds in its branches and roots! It's where the stories of gods, giants, and magical creatures all come together. The Vikings believed that as long as Yggdrasil stood tall, the universe would remain in balance, and life would continue to flow through the nine worlds. Even when Ragnarok, the end of the world, comes, some say that Yggdrasil will survive, sheltering new life and a new beginning for the realms it holds balanced.

Yggdrasil is truly a wonder—this ancient tree maintains all realms both balanced and connected, as well as supports creatures that remind us that the universe is full of mystery. Now that we know about this magical tree and its role in holding the worlds together, let's travel along its branches and visit some of these amazing realms, as well as learn about the secrets they hold, ourselves!

Asgard: Home of the Aesir Gods

Our first stop is back to Asgard, which you should remember to be the glorious home of the Aesir gods. It is one of the most important realms in Norse mythology. Let's glide past its golden halls gleaming in the sunlight, towering structures touching the sky, and magical beings walking among beautiful gardens in our ship. You will notice as you gaze out that Asgard is not just a city—it's a realm of wisdom, power, and endless adventure.

What Makes Asgard Special?

Asgard is where the most powerful community of gods lives, known as the Aesir. These include mighty Odin, the wise and mysterious Allfather, his son Thor, the protector of Midgard and wielder of the thunderous hammer Mjolnir, and Freya, the goddess of love, war, and beauty. It's a place where the air is always fresh, and the skies are filled with the glow of magic. Though the gods of Asgard are like a big family, they also have their fair share of squabbles (small arguments) and adventures.

Valhalla: The Hall of the Fallen

One of the most famous places in Asgard is Valhalla, Odin's great hall. Imagine a massive building with golden walls and a roof made of shining shields. Valhalla is where the Einherjar (INE-hair-yar), or the bravest warriors who died in battle, gather to prepare for Ragnarok, the end of the world. By day, the Einherjar train and fight, sharpening their skills for the final battle. By night, they feast on delicious meals and drink from magical cups that never run dry. It's a place where the party never ends, and every warrior is treated like a hero!

Bifrost: The Rainbow Bridge

Asgard is connected to the world of humans, Midgard, by the Bifrost, a magical rainbow bridge. Bifrost glows with all the colors of the rainbow and hums with energy as it stretches between realms. It's the only way to get to Asgard from the other worlds. As such, it's carefully guarded by Heimdall, a god with incredible senses. Heimdall has ears so sharp that he can hear the grass sprouting and even the wool growing on sheep! He keeps an eye out for any troublemakers—especially giants trying to sneak into Asgard.

Everyday Life in Asgard

Life in Asgard isn't just about battles and feasts. The gods have their own homes and halls, where they spend time planning, storytelling, and creating new wonders. Thor lives in Bilskirnir, the biggest house in Asgard, where he often invites friends over for feasts. Freyja rides across the sky in her chariot pulled by two giant cats, spreading beauty and magic wherever she goes. Odin is always seeking more knowledge, and sometimes he travels back to the roots of Yggdrasil to consult the wisdom of the Well of Mimir.

Asgard is a place where magic is woven into every corner. The gods often gather around the Well of

Urd, where the *Norns*—mysterious beings who control the fate of all living things—live. Here, the gods discuss the fate of the universe, share stories of their adventures, and make plans for the future.

Asgard is the heart of the Norse universe—a place where the gods make decisions that shape the fate of all the realms. It's a place of strength, wisdom, and sometimes mischief. The stories of Asgard remind us that even the mightiest heroes face challenges and that no matter how powerful you are, you still need friends by your side. It's a world where bravery, knowledge, and honor come together, showing us that true strength comes from standing up for what's right.

Are you ready to leave the golden halls of Asgard and explore the next realm? Let's step off our ship and onto Bifrost and continue our journey down to the world of humans, Midgard!

Midgard: The World of Humans

Unlike the magical realm of Asgard, Midgard is much closer to the everyday world we know today. It's where people live, work, and explore the mysteries of nature. But don't let its familiarity fool you—Midgard is filled with its own kind of magic, and the Vikings believed that their realm was also a place of great adventure and wonder.

Midgard means "Middle Earth" or "Middle Realm" in Old Norse. So naturally, this realm is located right in the center of the Viking universe. The name also comes from the fact that Vikings believed that Midgard is surrounded by a vast, uncharted ocean. To them, this ocean was the edge of the world. Beyond that, Midgard itself is a realm full of rolling hills, thick forests, tall mountains, and deep, mysterious oceans. It's a place where people live out their lives, building villages, farming the land, and sailing across the seas.

The Vikings saw Midgard as a place where nature was wild and untamed. They respected its power, from the roaring waves of the North Sea to the howling winds of winter storms. To the Vikings, every forest and fjord (long, narrow waterways that are surrounded by steep cliffs) could be home to magical creatures like elves, trolls, and spirits of the land.

The Giants' Threat

Even though Midgard is the realm of humans, it's not always peaceful. The Vikings believed that the sea surrounding Midgard was home to *Jormungandr*, the World Serpent. According to Viking legend, Jormungandr is so large that he can wrap around the entire world and bite his own tail! Though he normally slumbers beneath the waves, when he finally stirs he causes great storms and tsunamis. It is his very coils that shake the seas.

As the protector of Midgard, Thor often battles giants and monsters that threaten the human world. He's always ready to jump down from Asgard and fight off any giants or creatures that try to invade Midgard, keeping humans safe from harm. And, in return, the humans of Midgard honor Thor and the other gods in hopes of earning their favor and protection.

Midgard and Bifrost: The Bridge Between Gods and Humans

Midgard is connected to Asgard by a bridge called the Bifrost. As previously mentioned, the Vikings believed that even though the gods lived up in Asgard, they often visited Midgard to interact with humans. Thor would come down to protect humans from danger while Odin sometimes wandered through Midgard in disguise, searching for wisdom and testing the courage of mortals.

Loki, the trickster, also liked to come down to Midgard—though he often caused more trouble than he solved! Loki's tricks often led to big problems, but at times he also helped humans in unexpected ways. Even tricksters have a role to play in the world!

Life in the Viking Realm

For the Vikings, life in Midgard was full of challenges and opportunities. They farmed the land, raised animals, and built sturdy homes to keep out the cold northern winds. They were also expert sailors, and used their longships to travel across the seas in search of new lands, trading partners, or sometimes, enemies to raid.

The Vikings believed that everything in nature had a spirit. The forests, rivers, and mountains of Midgard were alive with creatures like *landvættir* (land spirits), who watched over certain places and protected them from harm. The Vikings respected these spirits and often left offerings for them, hoping these gifts would encourage the spirits to protect Viking villages.

So naturally, even though there were dangers brought with storms and wild beasts that roamed the land, the Vikings believed that Midgard was a place of great opportunity. It was where humans could prove their bravery and earn a place in Valhalla or *Folkvangr*, which was Freya's hall for the noble dead. Thus, a Viking's journey might have begun in a simple village, but they believed that courage and strength could make them legends.

Midgard's Connection to the Cosmos

The Vikings saw Midgard as a vital part of Yggdrasil (the World Tree) and vice versa. Not only did the Vikings believe that Yggdrasil's branches stretch over Midgard, offering a canopy of stars at night, they also thought that the roots of Yggdrasil, deep beneath the earth, connect Midgard to the underworld realms like Helheim. Beyond the twinkling light provided by Yggdrasil at night, the sky above Midgard also served as the space where the Vikings believed the gods were watching over the world. The thought that the gods were always present despite how far away they were reminded the Vikings that they were part of something much bigger than themselves.

The idea that Midgard was connected to Asgard through Bifrost further symbolized the close relationship between gods and humans. Whereas the gods influenced the fate of humans, the actions of humans could also impress or disappoint the gods. The stories of Midgard are filled with tales of humans meeting the gods, seeking their help, or challenging the gods to prove their strength and honor.

Why Midgard Matters

Midgard is special because it's the place where the stories of everyday people unfold. It's where heroes are made, families live and grow, and magic of the natural world comes alive. For the Vikings, Midgard was more than just a place—it was the center of their lives and their adventures. Even though we see it as our normal world, the Vikings knew that every river, mountain, and ocean held secrets waiting to be discovered.

Now that we've explored the world of humans, let's pack up our imaginary longship and head to a much wilder place—Jotunheim (YO-tun-hime), the land of giants! Are you ready for a little more danger and mystery? Let's continue our journey!

Jotunheim: The Land of Giants

Hold on tight, because now we're headed straight toward the wild and rugged land of Jotunheim where the giants roam! This realm is full of towering icy mountains, dark ancient forests, and swirling deep rivers, as well as creatures that could crush a house with their bare hands. Unlike the bright, orderly halls of Asgard, Jotunheim feels wild, mysterious, and even a bit dangerous.

Jotunheim is the land of the Jotnar, or giants, who are the ancient rivals of the gods of Asgard. The Vikings believed that the giants were powerful beings who could control nature itself. They could create snowstorms, earthquakes, and other natural disasters that could threaten the nine worlds. While not all giants were evil, many had a deep grudge against the gods, and they often plotted ways to cause trouble for Asgard.

The landscape of Jotunheim is so untamed that the Vikings said even the rivers here are made from the venom of giant snakes, which is why they are so wild and fast. Unlike the lush fields and beautiful gardens of Asgard, Jotunheim's scenery is rugged and raw, perfect for giants who enjoy their independence and freedom.

The Giants of Jotunheim:

The Jotnar, or giants, come in many shapes and sizes. Some are as tall as mountains, while others have strange features like many heads or the ability to change shape. The giants are as old as the world itself, and they possess ancient wisdom about the mysteries of the universe. But beware—not all giants are friendly!

Some giants, like Thrym and Skrymir, are known troublemakers. Thrym once stole *Mjolnir*, Thor's powerful hammer, and demanded Freya as his bride in exchange for returning it. But the gods weren't about to let that happen! Thor, disguised as a bride with Loki's help, managed to trick Thrym and win back his hammer.

On the other hand, not all giants are enemies of the gods. For example, a wise giant named Mimir lived near a magical well called Mimir's Well. Maybe you remember from before that Odin once visited Mimir's Well to gain wisdom, which cost him one of his eyes in exchange for a drink from its waters. So it's clear that even in Jotunheim, the gods could find allies and learn important lessons.

Jotunheim: A Land of Mysteries

Jotunheim is full of places that are shrouded in mystery and magic. Deep in its forests lie hidden caves, ancient ruins, and secret paths that only the bravest dare to explore. Some say that if you follow a certain river far enough, you might find a waterfall that leads to a secret valley where giants keep their treasure.

In Jotunheim, the nights are long, and the shadows are deep. Strange creatures roam the land, like frost giants who can create snowstorms with a single breath and mountain trolls that turn to stone when touched by sunlight. The giants' homes are carved out of the sides of cliffs, or hidden in the roots of giant trees, and they are filled with treasures from long-forgotten times.

But not everything in Jotunheim is scary. The realm also has beautiful, wild landscapes that stretch as far as the eye can see. The snow-covered peaks and crystal-clear lakes reflect the light of the stars, making Jotunheim a place where the sky feels close enough to touch. It's a place where nature rules, and even the gods must tread carefully in this world of untamed beauty.

Jotunheim is also the stage for some of the most dramatic battles in Norse mythology. In Norse mythology, Thor often visits Jotunheim, swinging Mjolnir as he protects Midgard from the giants' threats. His battles with the giants are the stuff of legend. And, every time he defeats a giant, it's a victory for the gods. Don't be fooled by these stories of triumph, however, as the giants are not easily defeated. Giants always seem to have new tricks and schemes up their sleeves.

Why Does Jotunheim Matter?

Jotunheim is a realm that reminds us of the wild, untamed parts of the universe—and of ourselves. It's a place not only where there are many challenges and dangers, but also where wisdom and hidden beauty thrive. It shows that even the most powerful beings, like the gods, have rivals they must face and mysteries they cannot easily understand. The giants and the gods may clash, but they are part of the same great story, each playing their role in the balance of the universe.

Jotunheim teaches us that not everything in life is neat and tidy. Sometimes, challenges come from unexpected places, and even those who seem like enemies have something to teach us. And though the giants may be fierce and stubborn, they are also a reminder that there is strength in standing tall, just like the mountains and trees of their homeland.

Now that we've braved the rocky peaks and deep forests of Jotunheim, let's continue our adventure to a place where nature and magic blend together perfectly—Vanaheim, the home of the Vanir gods. Ready for more magic and mystery? Let's go!

Vanaheim: Home of the Vanir Gods

It's time to step off the ship into the next realm. Let's explore Vanaheim (VAH-nuh-hime), the lush and magical realm where the Vanir gods live. While Asgard is full of great halls and buildings for the gods, Vanaheim is a land of natural beauty, where the gods are deeply connected to the cycles of nature, magic, and fertility. Imagine a realm where the rivers flow clear, the forests are filled with life. Every flower, tree, and mountain seems to hum with ancient magic here.

What Is Vanaheim?

Vanaheim is the home of the Vanir gods, who are, not surprisingly, known for their deep connection to nature, magic, and the mysteries of life. The Vanir are different from the Aesir gods of Asgard—they're more peaceful, focused on the magic of the earth, the sea, and the sky. While the Aesir are known for their strength in battle, the Vanir create balance due to their wisdom in growth, harvest, and enchantment.

Some of the most famous Vanir gods include Freya (Freyja) and her brother Frey, who now reside in

Asgard as previously mentioned. Another famous Vanir god is….

A Place of Nature's Magic

Vanaheim is like a magical, never-ending garden. Its forests are thick with trees that stretch up to the sky, and its meadows are filled with colorful flowers that bloom all year round. So, the Vanir gods live in harmony with the natural world. They use their powers to keep the seasons balanced, ensuring that crops grow in the summer and remain dormant (which is when crops rest) during the winter. Vanaheim is a place where the air is always fresh, and the land is always alive with the sounds of birds, insects, and rushing streams.

The rivers in Vanaheim are said to have magical properties. Some can heal wounds, others can reveal secrets to those who drink from them. There are hidden groves where time seems to stand still, and ancient trees that whisper the secrets of the universe to those who know how to listen. It's a place where every leaf and every stone has a story, and the Vanir gods understand how to listen to the language of nature.

Vanaheim's Mythical Creatures

But, Vanaheim is not just home to the Vanir gods—it's also filled with magical creatures that roam freely through its forests and fields. Some of these creatures are helpful, while others can be a bit mischievous! Remember the nature spirits (*landvættir*) that guard certain groves, streams, and hills? They also protect the land and sometimes bless or curse those who visit, depending on how they are treated.

In the deep woods, you might encounter *alfs*, light elves who love to dance and sing under the moonlight. These elves are said to have the power to heal, and they often share their knowledge of herbs and plants with the Vanir gods. The creatures of Vanaheim reflect the peaceful and enchanted nature of the realm, where everything seems to be touched by magic.

The Peace Treaty with Asgard

It's clear that Vanaheim and Asgard are very different realms. Where Vanaheim is full of nature and magic, Asgard is full of power and grandeur. So naturally, the residents of Vanaheim and Asgard weren't always allies. Long ago, the Vanir and the Aesir fought a great war. The Vanir, with their deep magic and knowledge of the earth, proved to be a strong match for the battle-hardened Aesir. But both sides eventually grew tired of the conflict, realizing that they were stronger together than apart. So, they made peace with each other and exchanged hostages to seal their alliance.

This is how Freyja and Frey, as well as their father Njord, came to live in Asgard with the Aesir. In return, the Aesir sent some of their own gods to Vanaheim, and the two realms began to learn from each other. Freyja and Frey brought their magic and wisdom to Asgard, helping to make it even more beautiful and prosperous. This exchange strengthened the bond between the two groups of gods and brought balance to the Nine Worlds.

Why Vanaheim Matters

Vanaheim is a realm that reminds us of the importance of living in harmony with nature. The Vanir gods teach the value of balance—between work and rest, between growth and renewal. While Asgard is a place of action and heroism, Vanaheim shows that there is strength in peace, patience, and understanding the rhythms of the natural world. The Vanir's wisdom helps ensure that the Nine Worlds stay in balance, and their alliance with the Aesir shows that cooperation can overcome even the longest of conflicts.

Vanaheim also teaches us that there is magic in everyday life—in the turning of the seasons, the growth of a plant, or the gentle breeze that carries the scent of flowers. For the Vikings, the Vanir represented the gentler side of the universe. These gods show us that not all power comes from might (strength)—some of it comes from the heart.

Now that we've explored the enchanting forests and peaceful fields of Vanaheim, let's move on to a realm that shines even more with magical light—Alfheim, the home of the elves. Are you ready to meet these mysterious, graceful beings? Let's continue our adventure!

Alfheim: Realm of the Light Elves

Our next stop on this magical voyage through the Nine Worlds is Alfheim (ALF-hime), the beautiful realm of the light elves. If you can imagine a place where sunlight dances through shimmering leaves, where rivers sparkle like diamonds, and where every flower glows with a gentle light, then you're starting to picture the wonders of Alfheim. The Vikings believed that Alfheim was home to beings of incredible beauty and grace, who lived in harmony with the natural world and wielded powerful magic.

What Is Alfheim?

Alfheim is the home of the light elves, or *Ljósálfar* (YOS-ahl-far). These magical creatures are known for their kindness, wisdom, and connection to the natural world. Unlike the dark and mysterious lands of Jotunheim, Alfheim is a realm of light and warmth. The light elves are often seen as protectors of nature, helping plants grow and guiding the rivers as they flow through the land.

The ruler of Alfheim is Frey (*Freyr*), one of the Vanir gods who moved to Asgard after the peace treaty between the Vanir and Aesir. As the god of fertility, sunshine, and prosperity, Freyr brings his joyful spirit to Alfheim. Though the elves look to Freyr as a leader, they live freely, dancing under the stars and celebrating the beauty of the world around them.

A Land of Enchantment

Alfheim is like a place out of a fairy tale, where everything is touched by magic. The forests of Alfheim are filled with trees that sparkle with dew and flowers that bloom in every color of the rainbow. When the sun shines through the leaves, it creates beams of light that make the air shimmer, creating a never-ending dance of light and shadow. The elves of Alfheim use their magic to keep the realm beautiful. To maintain their beautiful realm, they are known to sing songs that can make trees grow taller and flowers bloom even brighter.

The rivers of Alfheim are so clear that you can see the pebbles at the bottom, each one glowing with a gentle light. Some say that if you drink from an Alfheim river, you'll be blessed with a heart full of joy and dreams that are as bright as the stars. The lakes in Alfheim are so still that they reflect the sky perfectly, making it seem as if there are two skies— one above and one below.

The Elves of Alfheim

The light elves are known not only for their kindness, but also their love of dance, music, and storytelling. They live in elegant homes built into the sides of hills or high up in the trees, where they can watch the stars and listen to the songs of the wind. The elves often spend their evenings dancing in the moonlight or singing songs that tell the stories of ancient heroes and forgotten lands. Their voices are so beautiful that even the birds stop to listen.

The elves of Alfheim are also master healers, using their knowledge of herbs and plants to help those in need. If a traveler finds their way into Alfheim and is respectful to the elves, they might receive a gift of healing herbs or a blessing that protects them on their journey. But, the elves are also cautious—they are shy around strangers, and won't reveal their secrets to just anyone.

Elves and Their Magic

The powerful magic of the light elves comes from their deep connection to nature. They can speak to animals, summon gentle breezes, and even make flowers bloom with a wave of their hands. Some elves are said to be able to control the weather, calling forth gentle rains to water the forests or making the sun shine brighter on cold days.

The light elves use their magic to keep Alfheim in balance. They ensure that the trees, rivers, and animals of their realm all live in harmony. They can also use their magic to see into the future, just like the *Norns* who live near the roots of Yggdrasil. The elves often help the gods with their wisdom, and may share their knowledge of healing and nature with those who earn their trust.

Friendship with the Gods

As friends of the gods, the elves often visit Asgard. When they go to Asgard, the elves will bring flowers that bloom eternally and share songs that fill the halls of the gods with joy as gifts. In return, the gods respect the elves and protect Alfheim from any threats that might come from other realms, like the giants of Jotunheim or the fires of *Muspelheim (one of the Southern realms of Yggdrasil)*.

The elves also help the gods in their battles against the forces of chaos. During Ragnarok, the end of the world, it is said that the elves will stand beside the gods, shining like stars even in the darkest times. Their friendship with the gods shows that strength doesn't always come from muscle or weapons— sometimes, it comes from kindness, wisdom, and love for the world.

Why Alfheim Matters

Alfheim and its residents teach us about the beauty of nature and the magic that can be found in the simple things, like a flower blooming or a river flowing. The elves remind us that even the smallest creatures have a role to play in the world, and that kindness and gentleness can be just as powerful as strength and bravery. Alfheim is a place where dreams come alive, and where every tree, stream, and breeze carries a touch of magic.

For the Vikings, the light elves of Alfheim represented the beauty and mystery of the natural world. Their stories teach us to appreciate the wonders of the earth, to treat nature with respect, and to find joy in the world around us. Who knows—if you listen closely enough, you might even hear the soft singing of the elves when the wind blows through the trees!

Now that we've explored the enchanted forests and sparkling rivers of Alfheim, let's prepare ourselves for a much chillier adventure. Put on your warmest cloaks because our next stop is *Niflheim*, the realm of ice, mist, and freezing winds. Ready? Let's go!

Niflheim: Realm of Ice and Mist

Hopefully you've managed to bundle up, because our longship is heading south to Niflheim (NIF-el-hime), a realm that's as cold as it is ancient. Niflheim is a place where the ground is covered with frost, and rivers flow with icy water. It's one of the oldest realms in Norse mythology, and existed before many of the other worlds were created. If you can imagine a place where fog rolls over icy mountains, where glaciers stretch as far as the eye can see, and where the air is so cold that it bites at your skin, then you're starting to picture the frozen mystery that is Niflheim.

What Is Niflheim?

Niflheim means "Mist-Home" or "Mist-World" in Old Norse. Naturally, this is a realm of eternal cold and shadows. This icy world is home to *Hvergelmir* (HVAYR-gel-meer), a magical well or spring that is the source of many of the rivers that flow through the Nine Worlds. Hvergelmir is even said to bubble with icy waters that flow into great rivers like the *Gjöll* and the *Elivagar*, which are filled with cold, churning currents.

The air in Niflheim is filled with a thick, ghostly mist that makes it hard to see more than a few steps ahead. Sometimes, the mist glows with a pale blue light, casting eerie shadows on the frozen ground. The ground is covered with layers of ice and snow, and the winds howl through the canyons like a wolf on a cold winter night. Niflheim is a place of quiet and solitude, where even the bravest travelers can feel the weight of its ancient cold.

The Origins of Niflheim

Niflheim, alongside Muspelheim (the realm of fire), was one of the first realms that came into being. The Vikings believed that before the world as we know it was created,only the icy mist of Niflheim in the north and the searing flames of Muspelheim in the south existed. In between these two extreme realms lies a vast void called *Ginnungagap*. According to legend, when the cold of Niflheim met the heat of Muspelheim in the middle of Ginnungagap, something incredible happened—the ice melted, and from the drops of water emerged *Ymir*, the first giant, and *Audhumla*, the ancient cow that nourished him.

From these beginnings, the world of Norse mythology took shape. The first gods, including Odin, were born, and they eventually used Ymir's body to create the world. Niflheim's icy breath played a crucial role in this creation, making it a place of great importance in the stories of the Vikings.

The Well of Hvergelmir

Hvergelmir lies at the heart of Niflheim, and it is said to be the source of many of the rivers in the Nine Worlds. The water from Hvergelmir flows down through the roots of Yggdrasil, the World

Tree, feeding the life that stretches through the cosmos. Some of these rivers flow into the realms of men, bringing with them the cold breath of Niflheim.

Hvergelmir is also said to be home to *Nidhogg* (NID-hog), the terrible dragon who gnaws at the roots of Yggdrasil. Nidhogg is a fearsome creature, with scales as dark as midnight and eyes that glow like embers in the cold. He constantly bites at the roots of the World Tree in hopes of weakening it. His presence only adds to the eerie, dangerous feel of Niflheim. It is said that the icy waters of Hvergelmir help keep Nidhogg's hunger in check, but he never truly stops gnawing.

Creatures of the Mist
Niflheim might seem empty and desolate, but it has its share of mysterious inhabitants. Alongside Nidhogg, other creatures lurk in the misty shadows, like frost giants and ice spirits. These beings are as old as the ice itself, and they guard the secrets of the frozen realm. They are not quick to trust, and only the bravest adventurers can earn their respect.

The frost giants of Niflheim are different from the giants of Jotunheim. They are larger, quieter, and more solitary, spending their time wandering through the frozen wastelands. Some say that the giants' breath is what creates the swirling mists of

Niflheim, and that their footsteps can cause avalanches. The ice spirits, on the other hand, are small and swift, hiding among the glaciers and whispering through the icy winds.

Niflheim and Helheim: A Chilly Connection

Niflheim is closely connected to Helheim, the realm of the dead, which is ruled by Hel (Loki's daughter). Where Niflheim is a place of ice and mist, Helheim is a land of shadows and rest. It's said that some of the cold rivers that flow from Hvergelmir run through the borders of Helheim, maintaining the perpetual chill which is characteristic of the realm of the dead. Souls that find their way to Helheim pass through the misty edges of Niflheim, making this frozen world a gateway to the afterlife for those who did not die in battle.

But Niflheim itself is not a place where spirits linger for long. It's more like a threshold—a place between the realms of life and death, where the icy waters flow and the ancient dragon keeps his vigil. It is a world that serves as a reminder of the vast, cold forces that existed before the gods, and that will continue long after.

Why Niflheim Matters

Niflheim represents the power of cold, darkness, and mystery in Norse mythology. It teaches us that even in the harshest places, life can find a way. Niflheim reminds us that in the universe opposites maintain balance—as the cold of Niflheim and the heat of Muspelheim do. Niflheim's ancient, icy mists also serve as a reminder that the universe is much bigger and older than we can imagine, filled with secrets that we may never fully understand.

For the Vikings, Niflheim was a symbol of the unknown, of the dark winter nights when the cold seemed to stretch on forever. But it was also a reminder that the cold must be balanced with warmth and life, as it was Niflheim and Muspelheim together that helped create the world. Niflheim is a place that challenges the brave and inspires those who seek to understand the deepest mysteries of existence.

Now that we've braved the icy mists of Niflheim, let's warm up by journeying to a realm that's as hot as Niflheim is cold—Muspelheim, the land of fire! Ready to feel the heat? Let's go!

Muspelheim: The Realm of Fire

Brace yourself, because now we're traveling to Muspelheim (MOOS-pel-hime), a realm that's the complete opposite of Niflheim. It's time to take off those warm cloaks as quickly as possible because where Niflheim is a cold and misty world, Muspelheim is a land of roaring flames, scorching heat, and blazing volcanoes. Muspelheim is filled with fire giants and ruled by *Surtr* (SOOR-tur), a giant with a flaming sword. Legend has it that Sutr is destined to play a key role in Ragnarok, the end of the world.

What Is Muspelheim?

Muspelheim, or the "Land of Fire," is a realm that lies in the farthest reaches of the universe, where the air burns hotly and the ground is covered in rivers of molten lava. The Vikings believed that Muspelheim was one of the first realms to come into existence, alongside Niflheim. It is a place of raw, untamed energy, where the flames burn so brightly that they light up the dark skies of the Nine Worlds.

In Muspelheim, the land itself seems to be alive with fire. Volcanic eruptions shake the ground, sending fountains of lava high into the air. Great firestorms rage across the landscape, filling the sky with sparks and embers. Unlike the peaceful forests and rivers of realms like Alfheim or Vanaheim, Muspelheim is a place of constant motion and danger, where the heat is so intense that even the rocks glow with a fiery light.

Surtr: The Lord of Muspelheim

Surtr rules Muspelheim fearsomely with his sword that burns as brightly as the sun. Though Surtr's name means "black" or "the dark one," he is surrounded by flames that light up his shadowy figure. As one of the most powerful beings in Norse mythology, he guards the borders of Muspelheim. He is always ready to defend it against any who would dare enter.

Surtr's role in Norse mythology is closely tied to Ragnarok. The Vikings believed that when the time of Ragnarok comes, Surtr will lead the fire giants in an attack against the gods. He will use his flaming sword to set the world ablaze, burning everything in his path and bringing an end to the age of the gods. But from this destruction, a new world will be born, rising from the ashes like a phoenix.

The Fire Giants of Muspelheim

Surtr does not live alone on Muspelheim—he is joined by other fire giants, who are just as fierce and powerful as their ruler. Like their ruler, these giants are made of flame and shadow, with eyes that burn like coals and voices that crackle like burning wood. The fire giants of Muspelheim are warriors through and through, and they spend their time preparing for the great battle of Ragnarok.

The fire giants have little interest in the lives of humans or even the gods—Muspelheim is their domain, and they are content to let it burn. But their power is a constant threat to the rest of the Nine Worlds, especially since the fiery borders of Muspelheim lie so close to the void of Ginnungagap, where the first sparks of creation were born.

Muspelheim and the Creation of the World

Remember how Muspelheim played a crucial role in the creation of the world? After Ymir, the first giant, and Audhumla, the primeval cow were created, Ymir's body was later used by Odin and his brothers to shape the world. That means Muspelheim was one of the key forces that brought the universe into being.

This balance between fire and ice is at the heart of Norse mythology. The clash of these two elements is what started life, and their eventual battle in Ragnarok is what will bring an end to the current world. Muspelheim represents the destructive power of fire, but it also holds the potential for new beginnings.

Creatures of the Flame

Muspelheim is home to more than just fire giants—great flaming beasts also roam the burning plains, their bodies made of living fire. There are fire serpents that twist through the molten rivers, leaving trails of smoke behind them. Some stories even tell of fire spirits that dance through the flames like sparks, flickering in and out of sight.

These creatures are as wild and untamed as the flames themselves, and they guard the secrets of Muspelheim with a burning intensity. They are not easily tamed or befriended, but those who show respect for the power of fire may be able to learn from their wisdom. The fire spirits can reveal hidden paths through the mountains of Muspelheim or help guide travelers who are brave enough to explore the realm's dangerous depths.

Why Muspelheim Matters

Muspelheim represents the destructive and creative power of fire in Norse mythology, as fire can serve as both a force of destruction and a source of new life. The Vikings respected fire for its ability to warm their homes and cook their food, but they also feared its power to destroy and burn. Muspelheim is a reminder that even the most dangerous forces have a role to play in the balance of the universe.

For the Vikings, the flames of Muspelheim symbolized both the beginning and the end of all things. Just as the first sparks of creation came from Muspelheim's heat, so too will the final flames of Ragnarok consume the world, allowing for a new beginning.

Now that we've felt the heat of Muspelheim, let's cool back down as we explore Helheim, the realm of the dead, where shadows linger and spirits find rest. Are you ready for a journey into the land of quiet mysteries? Let's continue our adventure!

Helheim: Realm of the Dead

Now, let's step back off our longboat and into Helheim (HEL-hime), the shadowy realm of the dead. Helheim is a world unlike any other—a place of quiet, cold, and misty darkness where the spirits of those who did not die in battle find their final resting place. Here, Loki's daughter, Hel, rules over the souls that arrive in her realm. Helheim may sound a bit gloomy, but it's an important part of the

Viking understanding of life, death, and the afterlife.

What Is Helheim?

Helheim, unlike Valhalla (the hall of fallen warriors in Asgard), is the place where those who pass away from old age, sickness, or other natural causes go after they die. It is a somber realm where spirits find a peaceful, if somewhat chilly, rest. Here, rivers flow as silently as whispers and icy cliffs touch a pale, gray sky.

The Vikings thought Helheim was located deep underground, beneath the roots of Yggdrasil. It is said that to reach Helheim, a soul must travel down through the realms, past the borders of Niflheim, and cross the *Gjöll* river over a bridge guarded by the fearsome giantess *Modgud*.

Hel: The Queen of the Underworld

Hel, born of Loki and the giantess *Angrboda*, is a unique figure in Norse mythology—half of her body appears as a beautiful woman, while the other half is that of a skeleton, symbolizing her connection to both life and death. Though Hel is not cruel, she is stern and unyielding. She keeps a watchful eye over the souls that enter her realm, ensuring that they stay in Helheim and do not wander back to the world of the living.

Hel's hall (similar to the Viking concept of a palace) is called *Eljudnir*. Here in Eljudnir, she sits upon her throne, shrouded in mist. The Vikings believed that Hel's presence brought a sense of calm and order to her realm, making sure that the dead found peace. Though she offers comfort to those who accept their fate, there is a certain sadness in her eyes as she reflects on the mysteries of the afterlife.

Even though Hel might seem frightening at first, she plays a crucial role in maintaining the balance of the cosmos. Hel represents the natural cycle of life and death, reminding us that death is a part of life's journey, just as winter is a part of the changing seasons.

A Place of Quiet Rest

Helheim is a realm of stillness and eternal chill, where time seems to move more slowly. It's not a place of torment like the underworlds of some other cultures' mythologies, but rather a place of rest where spirits can sleep undisturbed. The souls here spend their time wandering among the quiet landscapes, reflecting on their lives and watching the soft fog roll over the hills.

VIKING & NORSE LEGENDS FOR KIDS

The land of Helheim is dotted with bare trees with branches covered in frost, and the ground is often frozen and hard. But even here, there is a quiet kind of beauty—icicles hang like crystals from rocky cliffs, and snowflakes fall silently from a gray sky. The spirits of Helheim move like shadows through this landscape, their steps leaving no trace in the snow.

In some stories, Helheim is home to the Hall of Mist, where the souls of the dead gather. It is a place where these souls can remember their lives and feel a sense of peace, even though they are far from the warmth of Midgard or the brightness of Asgard. It's a realm that offers a sense of closure to those who accept their fate and find comfort in the silence.

Helheim's Connection to Other Realms

Helheim is closely connected to Niflheim, the realm of ice and mist (remember that some of Helheim's icy rivers are even sourced from Niflheim). This is an important connection, as rivers like the Gjöll form a natural boundary between the world of the living and the realm of the dead. These boundaries make it difficult for any soul to leave once they have crossed over.

Helheim is also said to have a connection to the roots of Yggdrasil through one of its great roots.

This root stretches down into Helheim, drawing the life-giving waters of the well Hvergelmir and spreading them throughout the Nine Worlds. This root symbolizes the deep bond between life and death, showing that even the realms of the dead have a part to play in the cycle of existence.

Helheim's Role in Ragnarok

The Vikings believed that Hel and the inhabitants of Helheim will play a significant role in Ragnarok. Hel's realm will send forth an army of the dead, led by the great ship *Naglfar*, which is made from the nails of the deceased. This ship will sail into battle, carrying the spirits of those who have been waiting in Helheim for their chance to fight.

But, even in this moment of chaos, just as Muspelheim represents how flames can lead to both endings and new beginnings, Hel's presence is a reminder of the same. After the destruction of Ragnarok, when the world is reborn, the cycle of life and death will continue, and the balance between the realms will be restored.

Why Helheim Matters

Helheim teaches us about the importance of accepting the natural cycles of life and death. It's a place that shows that death is not something to be feared, but a part of the journey that all beings must take. For the Vikings, Helheim was a reminder of the inevitability of death. Though going here was not a punishment, Helheim also represented the importance of living a life of courage and honor while one still could, which would help with getting into Valhalla.

Even so, Helheim also shows that there is peace to be found even in the darkest places. It is a realm of quiet reflection, where souls can rest after a life well-lived. And while it might seem cold and lonely, Helheim is also a place where memories live on like whispers in the wind.

Now that we've explored the misty landscapes of Helheim, it's time to travel to another shadowy realm—*Svartalfheim*, the land of the dwarves. Now, it's time to light your torches so we can continue our journey!

Svartalfheim: Realm of the Dwarves and Dark Elves

Now, our longboat is docking at Svartalfheim (SVART-alf-hime), the mysterious realm of the dwarves (sometimes known as the home of the dark elves as well). Unlike the bright and shimmering land of Alfheim, Svartalfheim is a world of deep caverns, hidden mines, and twisting tunnels that stretch far beneath the earth. It's a place where shadows dance on the walls, and where treasures and secrets lie buried deep within the rocks.

What Is Svartalfheim?

Svartalfheim, which means "Home of the Black Elves" or "Home of the Dwarves," is a realm known for both its darkness and connection to the hidden powers of the earth. The Vikings believed that the dwarves were master craftsmen and smiths who could create incredible treasures using the metals and gems found deep underground. The realm is filled with forges (where people shape metal to create tools, weapons, and more) and workshops, where the air is always thick with the sound of hammers striking metal and the glow of furnaces lighting up the shadows.

The dwarves of Svartalfheim are known for their skill in creating magical items, weapons, and jewelry that are unmatched in quality. They crafted some of the most famous artifacts in Norse mythology, such as *Mjolnir*, Thor's hammer, *Gungnir*, Odin's spear, and *Draupnir*, a golden ring that produces eight new rings every ninth night. Their skills made them valuable allies to the gods, even though they preferred to live in their hidden world, away from the light.

The Dwarves of Svartalfheim

The dwarves are short, strong, and clever, with long beards and keen eyes that can see through the darkness of their underground home. They are known for being both stubborn and proud. Naturally, they take great pride in their work and have a deep respect for their craft. A dwarf's workshop is like a treasure trove, filled with tools, glowing embers, and half-finished projects made of gold, silver, and enchanted metal.

The dwarves are also known for their love of treasure. Their homes are often filled with piles of jewels, golden artifacts, and intricate carvings. But they do not share their riches lightly—those who wish to trade with or gain a gift from a dwarf must be prepared to show respect and offer something of equal value. The dwarves are not easily impressed, but they do admire those who show skill and determination.

Though they spend most of their time underground, the dwarves are aware of what goes on in the other realms. They sometimes trade with the gods, crafting weapons or offering their services in exchange for rare materials or magical favors. But be warned—if a dwarf feels cheated or tricked, they can be quick to anger, and they may find ways to take their revenge with a cunning trap or a tricky piece of magic.

The Hidden Treasures of Svartalfheim

Svartalfheim is a land of hidden treasures, where veins of gold, silver, and rare gemstones wind through the rocks like rivers. The dwarves know every secret path and every hidden chamber in their underground world. Deep in their mines, they dig for the rarest materials. For example, they look for materials like star metal, a magical substance that falls from the sky, and moonstone, which glows softly in the dark.

Some of the greatest treasures of Norse mythology were created in the forges of Svartalfheim. For example, when Loki once got into trouble with the gods, he turned to the dwarves of Svartalfheim to create gifts that would make amends. This is why the dwarves crafted Mjolnir, Thor's mighty hammer, which became the god's most trusted weapon. They also made *Skidbladnir*, a ship that can be folded up and carried in a pocket, and *Gullinbursti*, a golden boar that could run faster than any horse.

The process of creating these magical items is almost as enchanting as the items themselves. The dwarves use enchanted tools and ancient spells, shaping the metal with their hammers while singing songs that give the objects their magical powers. Watching a dwarf at work is like witnessing a magical ritual, where every strike of the hammer brings a piece of metal closer to becoming something extraordinary.

Creatures of the Shadows

Svartalfheim is not only home to dwarves; it is also sometimes associated with dark elves, mysterious beings who are said to live in the deepest parts of the earth. The dark elves are shadowy figures, known for their skill in weaving illusions and casting enchantments. Unlike the light elves of Alfheim, who love sunlight and laughter, the dark elves prefer the quiet darkness of their hidden world.

The dark elves can be both helpful and dangerous. They are masters of illusion, able to create shadows that move like living creatures and to disappear into thin air. Some say that the dark elves guard ancient secrets and forbidden knowledge, hidden in the darkest corners of Svartalfheim's labyrinthine caves. They might help travelers who show them respect, but they can also trick those who try to steal from their hidden vaults.

The presence of dark elves adds to Svartalfheim's mystery and danger. Even the dwarves, with all their knowledge, tread carefully around the places where the dark elves dwell. The shadows of Svartalfheim hold many secrets, and only those with a brave heart and a clear mind can hope to find their way through its hidden paths.

Why Svartalfheim Matters

Svartalfheim is a realm that represents the hidden forces of the earth—its treasures, its secrets, and its potential for creation and magic. It teaches us that some of the most powerful things in life are not always visible, but are hidden beneath the surface, waiting to be discovered. The dwarves remind us of the importance of skill, patience, and pride in one's work, while the dark elves remind us that the shadows can hold both wisdom and danger.

For the Vikings, Svartalfheim was a symbol of the unknown and the mysterious, a place where even the gods had to be cautious. It shows that there is strength in knowing how to craft, create, and explore the hidden corners of the world. And just as the dwarves dig deep into the earth for treasure, sometimes we have to dig deep within ourselves to find our own hidden strengths and talents.

Time to disembark our ship because we've now successfully journeyed through all of the Nine Worlds of Norse mythology together! From the shining halls of *Asgard* to the shadowy depths of *Svartalfheim*, each realm has its own mysteries, adventures, and characters that bring the world of the Vikings to life. I hope this exploration has been both fun and enriching, full of the magic and wonder that makes Norse mythology so captivating.

Did You Know?

- The Vikings believed that if you stood at the base of Yggdrasil, you could see all the nine worlds at once!

- Even though Loki causes trouble in Asgard, he's also known for traveling to many of the other realms to pull off his tricks.

With this knowledge in mind, let's continue our adventure and learn about the brave heroes and fearsome creatures that roam the Nine Worlds! Are you ready to hear more about Thor's battles, Loki's pranks, and the secrets hidden in these magical lands? Turn the page and let's dive into the tales that have been told for thousands of years!

CHAPTER 3:
HEROES OF VIKING LEGENDS

Welcome, young adventurer, and sit by the campfire as we tell stories about a land of brave warriors, daring explorers, and heroic deeds! The Vikings loved more than just their stories about gods and giants; they also told tales about heroes— people just like you if you're someone with some extra courage, strength, and a spirit for adventure than the average person. These heroes were the ones who faced terrible dragons, battled fierce monsters, and sailed across the ocean to discover new lands. Today, we're going to meet four of the most famous heroes of Viking legends. So it's time to grab your imaginary sword, put on a pair of sturdy boots, and journey through these thrilling stories!

Sigurd the Dragon Slayer: The Hero with a Magic Sword

Our first hero is *Sigurd*, a mighty warrior known for his bravery and his magical sword. He's one of the greatest heroes in all of Norse mythology, and his story is filled with magic, danger, and dragons!

Sigurd was raised by a wise blacksmith named *Regin*, who taught him how to forge weapons and fight with them. Regin had a secret, though—his brother, *Fafnir*, had turned into a terrifying dragon who guarded a mountain of treasure. Regin hoped that Sigurd would defeat Fafnir and claim the treasure, but he kept this plan hidden from Sigurd.

One day, Regin gave Sigurd a special task. He asked Sigurd to make a sword strong enough to defeat Fafnir. Sigurd made one sword after another, but they kept breaking. Finally, he melted down his father's old sword to make a new one called *Gram*. It was so sharp that it could cut through iron like butter!

With Gram in hand, Sigurd set out to face Fafnir. He dug a pit near the dragon's path and waited for the right moment. As Fafnir crawled over the pit, Sigurd leaped out and plunged his sword into the dragon's belly. With a mighty roar, Fafnir fell, and the ground trembled beneath his weight.

But the story doesn't end there! Regin told Sigurd to cook the dragon's heart and eat it. However, as Sigurd touched the heart, a drop of its blood fell onto his finger. When he licked the blood, something strange happened, as he could suddenly understand the language of birds! The birds warned Sigurd that Regin was planning to betray him and take all the treasure for himself (after Sigurd's hard work!).

Sigurd acted quickly, defeating Regin and therefore keeping the treasure. But he also took something with him that was even more valuable—wisdom, courage, and the knowledge that even a powerful hero needs to be careful about who to trust.

The story of Sigurd shows us that bravery can defeat even the fiercest monsters, and that wisdom is a hero's most powerful weapon. And who wouldn't want to hear the secrets of the birds?

Beowulf: The Mighty Warrior Who Battled Monsters

Now, let's march on to meet *Beowulf*, a hero whose story has been told for over a thousand years! Beowulf was known far and wide for his incredible strength and courage. He was the kind of hero who would face a dangerous monster without even breaking a sweat.

Beowulf's most famous adventure began when he traveled across the sea to help a kingdom in trouble. The kingdom was being terrorized by a terrible creature called *Grendel*, who would sneak into the great hall every night and cause chaos. Though the king and his warriors tried everything, they couldn't stop Grendel.

When Beowulf arrived, he promised the king that he would defeat Grendel, even though he didn't even bring a weapon! That's right—Beowulf decided to fight the monster with his bare hands. When Grendel attacked that night, Beowulf grabbed the creature's arm and wrestled with him. The fight was fierce, but Beowulf's strength was too much for Grendel. He tore off Grendel's arm, and the wounded monster ran back to his lair, never to bother the kingdom again.

However, Beowulf's adventure wasn't over yet! Grendel's mother, a powerful and angry sea witch, wanted revenge for her son. She attacked the king's hall, causing Beowulf to chase her to her underwater cave. He fought her in a battle beneath the waves, using a magical sword he found in her lair. With a mighty swing, he defeated her and brought peace to the kingdom.

Beowulf's story shows that true heroes never back down from a challenge, even when things seem impossible. And just like Beowulf, we can face our fears with courage, whether it's a scary monster or a difficult task at school!

Ragnar Lothbrok: The Legendary Viking King

Our next hero is *Ragnar Lothbrok*, a real Viking king whose story is as wild and adventurous as any myth! Ragnar was famous for his daring raids, his clever strategies, and his courage in battle. He was the kind of leader who could inspire his warriors to follow him anywhere—even to the ends of the Earth!

One of Ragnar's most famous adventures began when he decided to raid Paris (yes, the ancient version of the city we know today!), a mighty city surrounded by rivers and strong walls. The people of Paris thought their city was too well-protected for any army to conquer. But, they hadn't yet met Ragnar!

Ragnar gathered a fleet of longships and sailed up the river Seine with his warriors. He used his cleverness to trick the defenders of Paris. He pretended to be seriously ill and even arranged a fake funeral for himself. The defenders let his ship into the city, thinking he was no longer a threat. But when the time was right, Ragnar sprang from his ship, leading his warriors in a surprise attack! Thanks to his cunning plan, he managed to capture the city and win great treasure.

However, Ragnar's story didn't end there. He had many sons who became famous warriors too, like Ivar the Boneless, Bjorn Ironside, and Sigurd Snake-in-the-Eye. (yes, the same Sigurd who defeated the dragon!) They went on to explore new lands and continue Ragnar's legacy of adventure.

But Ragnar's story is also a lesson about pride. He once faced an enemy too powerful even for him— the king of Northumbria, who captured Ragnar and threw him into a pit of snakes. As the snakes surrounded him, Ragnar realized that even great heroes have their limits. His last words were a warning to his sons to seek vengeance, and his story lived on as a reminder that no one is invincible.

Ragnar's tale teaches us that being clever and brave can take you far, but it's also important to know when to be humble. Even so, he will always be remembered as one of the greatest Viking kings in history.

Stories of Viking Explorers: Erik the Red and Leif Erikson

Though Ragnar was known as a great king and warrior, not all Vikings followed in his footsteps—they were also amazing explorers who sailed farther than anyone thought possible! Two of the most famous Viking explorers include *Erik the Red* and his son, *Leif Erikson*. Though these men didn't fight dragons or monsters, they discovered new lands, making history with their courage and determination.

People called Erik "the Red" because of his fiery red hair and his bold personality. He was known for getting into trouble and being banished from his home in Norway. But instead of giving up after this punishment, Erik decided to go exploring westward across the icy seas. He discovered a huge, frozen island that he named *Greenland*. It wasn't very green, but Erik wanted to make it sound like a good place to live so he could encourage other Vikings to join him!

Erik settled in Greenland and built a new life there. But his biggest legacy was his adventurous spirit, which he passed on to his son, Leif Erikson.

Unsurprisingly, Leif Erikson took his father's love for exploration and ran with it. He had heard stories from sailors about lands even farther west than Greenland, so he set out to find them. After a long journey across the open ocean, Leif and his crew finally reached a place they called *Vinland*—which we now know as North America! It was a land filled with tall trees, wild grapes, and plenty of fish.

Leif Erikson and his crew built a small settlement in Vinland, making them the first Europeans to set foot in North America, nearly 500 years before Christopher Columbus! Although their settlement didn't last long, their incredible journey proved that there was a whole new world out there waiting to be explored.

Erik's and Leif's stories remind us that being an explorer takes a lot of bravery. They show us that sometimes, it's worth taking a risk to find out what's beyond the horizon. Thanks to their spirit of adventure, the Vikings are remembered not just as warriors, but as some of the greatest sailors and explorers in history.

Harald Hardrada: The Last Great Viking King

Now that we've highlighted some important Viking explorers, let's get back to the glories of battle. Our next story is about Harald Hardrada, who was a legendary Viking warrior and king of Norway. He is known as the "Last Great Viking King." His life was full of adventure, battles, and daring journeys that took him across Europe.

As a young man, Harald fled Norway and became a mercenary in the Byzantine Empire, where he gained fame for his bravery and strength. Harald fought in many battles, from the lands of Russia to the far-off city of Constantinople (modern-day Istanbul). With his accumulated wealth and reputation, he returned to Norway to claim the throne, becoming a powerful ruler. Harald was known for his ambition and desire to unite the Viking lands, dreaming of expanding his kingdom.

But, his story came to a dramatic end in 1066, when he tried to conquer England. He fought bravely at the *Battle of Stamford Bridge* against King Harold Godwinson. Despite his courage, however, he was defeated. Harald's death marked the end of the Viking Age, but his legacy as a fearless warrior lived on.

Harald's story teaches us about the determination to pursue our dreams, even when the challenges seem insurmountable. It also reminds us that though every era must come to an end, the stories of those who lived during it continue to inspire.

Grettir the Strong: A Hero Who Battled the Undead

Grettir the Strong was a famous Icelandic hero whose adventures are told in the *Saga of Grettir*. He was principally known for his incredible strength, stubbornness, but there is an interesting twist to his story; he is also known for being an outsider who never quite fit in with the other Vikings. Grettir's story is filled with both triumphs and hardships as he fought against trolls, ghosts, and other supernatural creatures.

One of Grettir's most famous battles was against a powerful *draugr*—a type of Viking zombie—named *Glam*. Glam was terrorizing a local farm, causing livestock to disappear and scaring the villagers. Grettir faced off with Glam in a fierce battle. Even though Grettir finally managed to defeat Glam, the undead creature cursed him before his death, bringing misfortune to Grettir's life.

This curse made Grettir's life difficult, as he found himself constantly at odds with others and he was unable to find peace. He became an outlaw, living alone in the harsh Icelandic wilderness. But even in exile, Grettir's strength and determination helped him survive. As such, he became a symbol of resilience and independence.

Grettir's story is a reminder that being different can be both a strength and a challenge. His battles against monsters and his struggles to find his place in the world show that true strength comes from within, even when the odds are against you.

These heroes—Sigurd the Dragon Slayer, Beowulf the mighty warrior, Ragnar Lothbrok the legendary king, the daring explorers Erik the Red and Leif Erikson, Harald Hardrada the last great Viking king, Brynhild the courageous Valkyrie, and Grettir the Strong—show us that there are many ways to be brave. Whether they were slaying monsters, facing tragic love, outsmarting enemies, exploring new lands, or battling the forces of the undead, each of them had a special kind of courage that made their stories worth telling.

Maybe you, too, have a bit of a Viking hero inside you! Like Sigurd, you can face challenges with bravery. Like Beowulf, you can fight for what's right. Like Ragnar, you can lead others with courage and cleverness. Like Erik and Leif, you can explore new places and discover amazing things about the world. Like Harald, you can strive for greatness, even when the odds are against you. Like Brynhild, you can follow your heart, no matter where it leads. And like Grettir, you can find strength within yourself, even in the toughest times.

So, what's your next adventure going to be? The world is waiting, so it's time to find the spirit of the Vikings in you!

Did You Know?

- The Viking longships were so well-built that they could sail across oceans or sneak up rivers, making the Vikings great explorers!

- In Viking stories, dragons were often a symbol of greed and danger. That's why defeating a dragon, like Sigurd did, was considered a great achievement.

- Leif Erikson Day is celebrated on October 9th in honor of the first European to reach North America!

CHAPTER 4:
MYTHICAL CREATURES AND BEASTS

———— ✦◇◇◉◇◇✦ ————

Welcome, young adventurer, to the land of mythical creatures, where giant beasts roam, magical horses gallop across the skies, and mysterious beings lurk in forests and caves. In Viking legends, the world was filled with all kinds of strange and magical creatures—it's true that some were friends, and others were foes, but even so, all of them had incredible stories to tell. Today, we're going to meet some of the most fascinating creatures from Norse mythology. So grab your adventurer's pack, and get ready for a journey into a world where anything is possible!

Fenrir the Wolf: The Beast Who Defies the Gods

Our first creature is *Fenrir*, the most fearsome wolf in all of Norse mythology. Fenrir was no ordinary wolf—he was a giant, with fangs as sharp as swords and a howl that could shake the mountains. He was so big that when he opened his mouth, he could swallow the sun! But Fenrir wasn't always a monster. He started out as a tiny wolf pup, but he grew bigger and more dangerous every day.

You should remember that Fenrir was the son of Loki, the trickster god, and a giantess named *Angrboda*. This meant that from the beginning, he had a wild side. The gods of Asgard, like Odin and Thor, knew that Fenrir would become a threat, so they decided to keep an eye on him. But as Fenrir grew bigger, they realized that no chain could hold him!

The gods tried to trick Fenrir into wearing a magical chain called *Gleipnir*. Gleipnir was made from things like the sound of a cat's footsteps, a woman's beard, and the roots of a mountain! It was thin and smooth like a ribbon, but stronger than steel. The gods told

Fenrir it was a game and challenged him to break the chain. But Fenrir, being clever, sensed a trick. He agreed to the challenge only if one of the gods put their hand in his mouth as a sign of trust.

Brave *Tyr*, the god of war, stepped forward and put his hand in Fenrir's mouth. When the chain tightened around Fenrir and he realized he couldn't break free, he bit off Tyr's hand! Even though the gods had captured Fenrir, they knew he would break free during Ragnarok to seek his revenge. During the end of the world, it was said that Fenrir would break his chains, fight Odin, and bring chaos to the world.

Fenrir's story is both thrilling and scary. It teaches us that even the mightiest heroes sometimes have to face challenges they can't completely control. And it reminds us that sometimes, even creatures that start small can grow into something much bigger and more powerful!

Jormungandr: The World Serpent That Encircles the Earth

Next, let's meet *Jormungandr*, also known as the "Midgard Serpent." Jormungandr is another child of Loki and Angrboda, and he's even more mysterious than Fenrir! He's a giant sea serpent so huge that he wraps all the way around Midgard, which is why he's sometimes also called the "World Serpent."

Jormungandr lives deep beneath the ocean. As he twists and turns, he creates powerful waves. Furthermore, the Vikings believed that when Jormungandr wriggled in his sleep, he caused earthquakes and storms at sea. Sailors often prayed to Thor to keep them safe from the serpent's mighty movements.

One of the most famous stories about Jormungandr is about his great battle with Thor. Thor once went fishing with a giant named *Hymir*, but instead of catching a regular fish, he hooked Jormungandr! Thor pulled and pulled, and the serpent's enormous head rose out of the water, dripping with seawater and poison. The two stared each other down, and Thor raised his hammer, Mjolnir, to strike the serpent. But just as he was about to deliver the final blow, Hymir cut the fishing line, and Jormungandr disappeared back into the ocean's depths.

But this won't be the last time they meet. During Ragnarok, it was foretold that Jormungandr and Thor would face each other again in a battle so fierce that it would shake the heavens and the earth. Though it was said that Thor would defeat the serpent, he would only be able to take nine steps before Jormungandr's poisonous breath would claim his life.

Jormungandr's story reminds us that sometimes, the biggest challenges are hiding right beneath the surface. And, like Thor, we need courage to face whatever might be lurking in the deep!

Sleipnir: Odin's Eight-Legged Horse

Now, let's meet a creature who is a little less scary but just as amazing—*Sleipnir*, Odin's eight-legged horse. But, not only are Sleipnir's legs unique to him, as he is the fastest and most powerful steed in all the nine realms! With his eight legs, Sleipnir can gallop across the sky, glide over the sea, and even travel between the different worlds in the blink of an eye.

Just like his eight legs, Sleipnir's story is a bit strange. He was actually the child of Loki—yes, that same mischievous trickster—and a magical stallion. One day, a builder offered to help the gods build a great wall around Asgard to protect them from giants. But the gods made a deal that if this builder didn't finish the wall on time, he wouldn't get paid. The builder had a powerful horse that was helping him work very quickly, so Loki turned himself into a mare (a female horse) to distract the stallion. Well, it worked a little too well, and Loki ended up giving birth to Sleipnir!

Even though Loki's plan was pretty wild, Odin loved Sleipnir and claimed this odd creature for himself. So, whenever Odin needs to travel across the worlds, he rides Sleipnir, whose eight legs make him faster than any other horse. Sleipnir is not only strong and swift, but also loyal to Odin, carrying him into battles and across the sky.

Sleipnir's story teaches us that sometimes, the strangest things can turn out to be the most special. And who wouldn't want to ride a magical horse that could take you anywhere in the universe?

The Valkyries: Warrior Maidens of the Battlefield

Let's move on from special creatures to a set of powerful women called the *Valkyries*. Remember Brynhild from before? If you do, you probably already know that the Valkyries are Asgard's squad of fierce warrior maidens. The Valkyries answer to Odin, flying over battlefields in shining armor and carrying fallen warriors to *Valhalla*, the great hall of the brave.

The name *Valkyrie* means "chooser of the slain," and that's exactly what they did. During battles, the Valkyries would decide which warriors were brave enough to join Odin in Valhalla. Remember that after reaching Valhalla, these warriors, known as the *Einherjar*, would spend their days training for the final battle of Ragnarok and their nights feasting with the gods.

But, the Valkyries did more than just bring the slain to Valhalla—they were also fierce warriors! As such, these women symbolized honor and bravery in Viking culture. The Vikings believed that if you fought bravely enough in battle, a Valkyrie might not only choose you to go to Valhalla, but also to ride with her there. Imagine soaring through the sky on a Valkyrie's winged horse, heading to a place where heroes feast forever!

The Valkyries remind us that true heroes should never give up, even when the odds are against them, as bravery and honor are always rewarded.

Trolls, Dwarves, and Elves: Friends and Foes of the Vikings

Our last stop is the magical world of trolls, dwarves, and elves. These beings live in the shadows and forests of different Viking worlds. Where some of them are friendly, others are a little more troublesome!

Trolls are giant creatures that live in the mountains and caves of Jotunheim. They can be tricky and grumpy, especially when humans or gods get too close to their homes. Trolls don't like sunlight, and if the sun's rays touch them, they turn to stone! So, they come out mostly at night, lurking in the shadows. But not all trolls are mean—some are just lonely and curious about the world outside their caves.

Dwarves, as you should remember, are small but mighty creatures who live deep underground in *Svartalfheim*. They are master blacksmiths and craftsmen, creating the most powerful weapons and magical items in all the nine realms. Dwarves might be grumpy and like to keep to themselves, but they're always up for a challenge, especially if it means making something new and amazing!

Elves come in two kinds: the *light elves* and the *dark elves*. You should recall that the light elves live in *Alfheim*. They are beautiful, graceful creatures who love music, dance, and magic. These elves are friendly and often help humans with their knowledge of healing and nature. Careful not to get them confused with the dark elves though, who prefer the shadows of *Svartalfheim* and can be a bit more mischievous, hiding away underground..

These creatures remind us that the world is full of surprises, and sometimes, the most magical things can be found in the places we least expect. Whether it's a grumpy troll, a clever dwarf, or a graceful elf, each of them has their own special role in the Viking world.

Hugin and Munin: Odin's Raven Messengers

Though *Hugin* (HOO-gin) and *Munin* (MOO-nin) are not fearsome beasts like Fenrir or Jormungandr, they are no less important. You may recall that these two ravens are the trusted companions of Odin, and they help him keep watch over the nine realms. Their names mean *Thought* (Hugin) and *Memory* (Munin). So naturally, they fly across the world every day, gathering news and secrets.

Hugin and Munin perch on Odin's shoulders and whisper into his ears, telling him everything they have seen and heard. This is how Odin knows what's happening in the world of humans, in Asgard, and beyond. The ravens are swift and clever, and nothing escapes their watchful eyes.

The Vikings saw ravens as symbols of wisdom and knowledge, and they believed that these birds had a special connection to the divine. Hugin and Munin remind us that sometimes, the smallest creatures can have the biggest impact, especially when they help us see the world more clearly.

Garm: The Guardian of Helheim

Garm is a monstrous hound that guards the gates of *Helheim*, the realm of the dead. He is sometimes called the "Hellhound," and is known for his ferocious strength and his ability to sense those who approach the underworld. His coat is stained with the blood of the souls he has faced, and his howls echo through the misty lands of Helheim.

During *Ragnarok*, it is foretold that Garm will break free from his chains and join the battle against the gods. He is destined to fight *Tyr*, the one-handed god of war, in a fierce struggle where both will meet their end. Garm's story is a reminder that even the fiercest guardians have their role to play in the great cycle of life and death.

And there you have it, adventurer—a tour of the most amazing mythical creatures and beasts from Norse mythology! Each one has its own story, filled with excitement, danger, and a touch of magic. From Fenrir's wild howl to Sleipnir's galloping hooves, these creatures make the Viking world a place of endless adventure.

Which one would you like to meet? Would you ride across the sky on Sleipnir, chat with an elf in Alfheim, or join a Valkyrie on her journey to Valhalla? The choice is yours, and the stories are waiting to welcome you!

Did You Know?

- The name *Jormungandr* means "huge monster" in Old Norse—pretty fitting for a serpent that can wrap around the entire world!

- In Viking times, people carved runes on stones to honor brave warriors, hoping that the Valkyries would carry them to Valhalla.

- Some stories say that trolls still roam the mountains of Norway, hidden away in caves and waiting for nightfall.

Now that you know all about these incredible creatures, are you ready to hear the stories of the epic battles they fought and the gods they encountered? Time to turn the page and see what adventures await in the next chapter!

CHAPTER 5: THE EPIC ADVENTURES OF THOR AND LOKI

It's time to embark on our next adventure. This journey will be filled with excitement, laughter, and danger, as we follow two of the most famous gods in Viking mythology—Thor and Loki. As you should now know, Thor is always ready to defend the world from giants and monsters with his powerful hammer, Mjolnir, and fierce spirit. Loki, on the other hand, is a trickster who loves playing pranks and stirring up trouble, even when it lands him (and sometimes others) in hot water. Together, they've had some of the most thrilling adventures in all of Norse mythology. So, hold on tight as we explore the tales of their greatest exploits!

Thor's Battle with the Giants of Jotunheim

As you well know by now, in many legends Thor must often travel to *Jotunheim* to keep the giants in check. The giants were known for causing trouble, but they were never too happy when Thor showed up with *Mjolnir*, ready to challenge them. So naturally, Thor had many battles with the giants, but one of the most famous is the story of how he fought *Hrungnir*, the strongest giant of all.

One day, Hrungnir bragged that he was so strong that no one could defeat him, not even the gods of Asgard. Hearing this, Thor became furious. He challenged Hrungnir to a duel, and they agreed to meet at the border between Asgard and Jotunheim. Hrungnir, being a giant, was enormous, and he carried a shield and a huge stone weapon called a "whetstone." Despite his size, power, and weapons, Thor was not afraid of Hrungnir. He trusted that Mjolnir would help him win the battle.

When the fight began, Hrungnir threw his whetstone at Thor, but Thor swung Mjolnir with all his strength. The two weapons collided in mid-air with a thunderous crash! Mjolnir first shattered the whetstone into tiny pieces, and then it struck Hrungnir. Thor's hammer had defeated the giant with one mighty blow. But a shard of the whetstone got lodged in Thor's forehead, and it stayed there for the rest of his life.

After the battle, the giants in Jotunheim knew better than to challenge Thor again. Thor's bravery and strength reminded everyone that no matter how big the challenge, you can always overcome it with courage and a strong heart. And while the whetstone in his forehead gave him a bit of a headache, Thor wore it as a reminder of his victory over the mighty giant!

Loki's Tricks and the Punishment That Followed

Now let's switch gears to talk about Thor's mischievous brother, Loki. You should recall from the many legends we've already discussed that Loki is quite the trickster—he loves to play pranks and create mischief, even when it's not always a good idea. One of Loki's most famous pranks involved the goddess *Sif*, who had long, golden hair that everyone admired.

One day, Loki decided it would be hilarious to sneak into Sif's bedroom while she was sleeping and cut off all her hair! When Sif woke up, she was devastated, and her husband(who was, coincidentally, Thor) was furious. Thor grabbed Loki and threatened to crush every bone in his body unless he fixed the mess he'd made. Loki, realizing he had gone too far, promised to make things right.

Loki went to the dwarves, the best craftsmen in the nine worlds, and asked them to create a magical wig for Sif. The dwarves made a beautiful new head of hair for Sif, woven from real gold, which shimmered even more brightly than her original hair. But Loki, being Loki, couldn't resist playing another trick. He made a bet with the dwarves, challenging them to make even more magical treasures. If they succeeded, Loki promised to give them his head. But if they failed, they would owe him a great prize.

The dwarves accepted the challenge and created amazing gifts: a magical ring that multiplied gold, a ship that could fold up small enough to fit in a pocket, and even Thor's hammer, Mjolnir!. Loki tried to cheat during the contest, but the dwarves saw through his trickery. They finished their creations, and Loki lost the bet.

But when the dwarves came to collect Loki's head, he found a loophole! He told them they could take his head but not touch his neck. The dwarves realized they couldn't take Loki's head without cutting his neck, so they settled for sewing his lips shut instead! So, for a while Loki had to stay quiet, as he was unable to tell any more lies or play any more tricks. But don't worry, he eventually got those stitches off and went right back to his mischief!

Loki's story teaches us that tricks and jokes can be fun, but they can also have consequences. It's always important to think about how our actions might affect others before we play a prank.

The Tale of Mjolnir and How It Was Both Lost and Found

Mjolnir was, unsurprisingly, Thor's most prized possession. This hammer was so powerful that it could not only create thunder and lightning, but also smash mountains with a single blow. But there was a time when Mjolnir went missing, and Thor had to go on a wild adventure to get it back.

One morning, Thor woke up and reached for Mjolnir, but it was gone! He searched everywhere, but the hammer was nowhere to be found. Thor was furious and immediately suspected the giants. He called on Loki for help, and together they went to *Jotunheim* to find out what had happened.

When they arrived, they discovered that *Thrym*, the king of the giants, had stolen Mjolnir and buried it deep underground. Thrym made a deal with Thor—he would only return the hammer if the gods gave him Freya, the beautiful goddess of love, to be his bride.

When Thor and Loki told Freya about the giant's demand, she was so angry that the ground shook beneath her feet. She refused to marry Thrym, so Thor and Loki came up with a clever plan. They decided that Thor would dress up as Freya in a wedding dress and go to Jotunheim to trick the giant.

Thor wasn't too happy about wearing a dress, but he agreed to the plan for the sake of his beloved hammer. Loki disguised himself as a bridesmaid, and together they traveled to Jotunheim for the "wedding." When they arrived, Thrym was so excited to meet his bride that he didn't even notice how tall and muscular "she" was!

At the wedding feast, "Freya" (Thor in a dress) ate an entire ox, eight salmon, and three barrels of mead! Thrym was surprised at the bride's enormous appetite, but Loki explained that "Freya" hadn't eaten for days because she was so excited to marry him. Finally, Thrym brought out Mjolnir to bless the marriage, placing it on "Freya's" lap.

As soon as Mjolnir was in Thor's hands, he threw off the wedding veil and revealed his true identity! He swung Mjolnir and defeated Thrym and the giants, taking back his hammer. With Mjolnir safely in his grasp, Thor and Loki returned to Asgard, laughing all the way home about their wild adventure.

This story shows that sometimes, even the mightiest hero needs a little creativity and humor to solve a problem. And, it's a good reminder that a great disguise can come in handy when you're dealing with tricky giants!

These epic adventures of Thor and Loki are filled with battles, pranks, disguises, and tricks. They show us that even the gods have to think on their feet and use their wits to solve problems. Thor's bravery and strength, paired with Loki's cleverness (and a bit of mischief), make them an unforgettable team.

Which story did you like best? Was it the time Thor dressed up as a bride to get his hammer back? Or the thrilling battle between Thor and the giants? Maybe it was Loki's tricks and the lessons he learned when he got caught? Whatever your favorite, these tales remind us that adventure is always around the corner, especially when you have friends (or brothers) like Thor and Loki!

Did You Know?

- Mjolnir means "Lightning" in Old Norse, and it was believed that this natural phenomenon protected both gods and humans from danger.

- The story of Thor's lost hammer is called *Thrymskvida*, one of the funniest tales in Norse mythology!

Now that you've heard about Thor and Loki's wild adventures, are you ready to learn about the real people who believed and created these stories? Turn the page and let's continue our journey through the incredible world of the Vikings!

CHAPTER 6: RAGNAROK - THE END OF THE WORLD

————————◆◇◇◉◇◇◆————————

Hello again, young adventurer! After exploring the nine realms and their involvement in Ragnarok, let's dive into the most dramatic and exciting chapter of Norse mythology—the end of the world itself! As you must remember from the tales of the nine worlds, the Vikings foretold of a huge battle that would change everything. Imagine a world where the skies turn dark, the oceans rise, and even the gods themselves fall in battle. But don't worry— this story isn't all about destruction. At the end of Ragnarok, there's a glimmer of hope, a chance for a new beginning. So, grab your sword and shield, and let's find out what happens when the Viking world faces its greatest challenge!

What Is Ragnarok? A Prophecy of Doom

Ragnarok (pronounced RAHG-nuh-rahk) is a word that means "fate of the gods." It's the Viking version of the apocalypse—a time when everything the gods have built begins to crumble, and the universe faces its greatest test. The Vikings believed that Ragnarok was foretold by prophets and seers—people who could see into the future and warn the gods about what was coming.

The story of Ragnarok begins with a series of strange and terrible events called the *Fimbulwinter*. The Vikings believed that this would be a winter like no other—lasting for three long years with no summer in between. In this legend, snow and ice would cover the land, crops won't be able to grow, and people will struggle to survive. The wolves *Skoll* and *Hati*, who chase the sun and moon, will finally catch up and devour them, plunging the world into darkness.

During this time, the bonds that held back Loki's monstrous children will begin to break. The great wolf *Fenrir* will escape from his chains, and the World Serpent, *Jormungandr,* will stir restlessly in the ocean, creating huge waves that will flood the land. Even *Hel*, ruler of the underworld, will be prepared to send the spirits of the dead to join the final battle.

The gods of Asgard knew that Ragnarok will come, and they have thus prepared for war. Odin has consulted with his ravens, Huginn and Muninn, and even went to seek wisdom from the head of *Mimir*, a talking head that knew many secrets. But no matter what they have done, they can't stop the prophecy from unfolding. The sky itself will split open, and the giants of *Jotunheim* will march towards Asgard, led by *Surtr*, the giant with a flaming sword.

Ragnarok will be the time for the final battle—a battle that will decide the fate of the world.

The Great Battle: Gods vs. Giants

Stories recount that the battlefield of Ragnarok will stretch across the heavens and the earth. On one side the gods of Asgard will stand—Odin, Thor, Freya, Tyr, and many more, ready to defend their home. On the other side will come the giants, led by Surtr, whose fiery sword lights up the sky like a second sun. Fenrir, Jormungandr, and the armies of Hell will join the giants, turning the battle into a clash of fire and ice.

Odin, the Allfather, will lead the charge on his eight-legged horse *Sleipnir*. He will face Fenrir, who he had once tried to chain. Fenrir will open his enormous jaws, and it was said that his mouth can stretch from the ground all the way up to the sky. Odin will fight bravely, but even his wisdom and strength can't defeat the monstrous wolf. With a snap of his jaws, Fenrir is sure to swallow Odin whole, and the Allfather will fall.

But Odin's son, *Vidar*, will be watching. Vidar is known as the silent god, but when he sees his father fall, he will be filled with rage. He will grab Fenrir's jaws, one with each hand, and tear them apart, avenging his father's death. Even in this dark moment, the gods will show their courage and strength.

Meanwhile, Thor will face his greatest enemy—Jormungandr, the World Serpent. Though Thor and Jormungandr have met before, this time it will be a fight to the end. Thor will swing his mighty hammer, *Mjolnir*, and strike the serpent with all his strength. The blow is foretold to be so powerful that it will shatter mountains and make the earth tremble. Jormungandr will ultimately be defeated, but as the serpent dies, it will release a poisonous breath that fills the air. Legend has it that Thor will take nine steps back before he falls, overcome by the deadly poison.

Loki, the trickster god, will fight against *Heimdall*, the watchman of Asgard. The two have always been enemies, and now they will face each other in a battle of wits and strength. Their fight will be fierce and balanced, with neither gaining the upper hand. But in the end, legend has it that they will strike each other down at the same time, and both Loki and Heimdall will fall to the ground, never to rise again.

As the gods and giants clash, Surtr will raise his flaming sword and set the world on fire. Flames will engulf the earth, and the sky will turn red. It was foretold that the heat will melt mountains, and the sea will boil with steam. The great tree *Yggdrasil* shall shake, and its branches crack as the universe itself begins to fall apart.

It will seem like everything was lost. During Ragnarok, the gods will have fallen, the world will burn, and darkness will have covered the land. But even in the midst of all this destruction, a new hope will be waiting to be discovered.

The Death of Odin, Thor, and Loki

The loss of Odin, Thor, and Loki would have been a great tragedy for the Viking world. Odin, the wise ruler of the gods, had always guided Asgard with his knowledge and wisdom. Thor, the protector of Midgard, had fearlessly defended humans from giants and monsters. And even Loki, with all his tricks and mischief, had played an important role in the stories of the gods.

But the deaths of these powerful figures were not the end of their stories. In Viking belief, death simply represented a part of the cycle of life, and even the greatest heroes would one day meet their fate. The Vikings believed that after a warrior fell in battle, they would join the spirits of the brave in *Valhalla*, feasting and fighting until the end of time. The deaths of Odin, Thor, and Loki would symbolize the coming of a great change, a new age when the old world would give way to a fresh start.

The Rebirth of the World: A New Beginning After the End

Just when it may have seemed like everything had been destroyed in Ragnarok, something amazing is foretold to happen—a new world will begin to grow from the ashes. The fire that had burned the earth will slowly die down, and the flames will give way to new green shoots. The earth shall rise from the sea, fresh and clean, and life will begin again.

From the roots of Yggdrasil, two humans named *Lif* and *Lifthrasir* will emerge. They had been hiding in the World Tree during Ragnarok, meaning they would be the only people left to repopulate the world. Lif and Lifthrasir shall walk across the new earth, marveling at the green fields, the clear rivers, and the bright sun that shines in the sky.

A few of the gods will have survived the great battle too. *Balder*, the god of light who had been killed before Ragnarok, will return from the underworld, bringing hope and peace to the new world. Vidar, the avenger of Odin, and *Magni* and *Modi*, the sons of Thor, will find Mjolnir and continue their father's legacy. Together, they will help to rebuild the world and ensure that the mistakes of the past are not repeated.

The Vikings believed that this new world would be a place of peace and happiness, where people and gods could live together without fear of giants or monsters. The sun will shine again, and the stars will twinkle in the sky. Animals will roam freely, and the waters will be full of fish. It will be a chance for the world to start fresh.

The story of Ragnarok reminds us that even when everything seems dark, there is always hope for a new beginning. It teaches us that every ending is the start of something new, and that even the greatest challenges can lead to something beautiful. The cycle of life, death, and rebirth was at the heart of the Vikings' beliefs, and it gave them the strength to face whatever challenges came their way.

A Tale of Courage, Change, and Hope

The story of Ragnarok is one of the most powerful tales in Norse mythology. It is a story of brave gods and fierce battles, of loss and sacrifice, but also of renewal and hope. For the Vikings, this story wasn't just a tale of doom; it was a reminder that even in the darkest times, the spirit of adventure, courage, and honor would always live on. They believed that while the world might change, and the gods might fall, their bravery and values would endure, inspiring future generations to face their own challenges.

In the heart of the tale lies the message that no matter how difficult or scary a situation may seem, facing it with courage is what truly matters. The gods of Asgard knew that they wouldn't be able to prevent Ragnarok—they couldn't change their fate—but they would still choose to face the final battle with all their might. They will fight with every ounce of strength they have, knowing that their actions will echo through time. This kind of bravery was what the Vikings admired most, and it's why they told the story of Ragnarok to their children, hoping to teach them the same lessons about facing life's challenges with courage.

Keeping the Spirit Alive: The Power of Stories

Even though some Vikings believed that the gods of Asgard had already fallen during Ragnarok, while others thought that Ragnarok was yet to come, the stories of the gods continued to be told around the fires of Viking villages. The Vikings passed down the tales of Odin's wisdom, Thor's strength, and Freya's compassion, teaching each new generation about the values that made the gods so great. These stories became a source of strength for the Vikings, reminding them that even in difficult times, they could find the courage to carry on.

Imagine a cold winter night, with snow covering the ground and the wind howling outside. Inside a warm longhouse, a family gathers around the fire, listening as the village *skald* (storyteller) recounts the story of Ragnarok. Even as they hear about the great battles and the loss of their beloved gods, they also hear about the new world that was born from the flames, where life could begin again. These stories gave them hope and made them feel connected to their ancestors, their heroes, and the cycle of life.

And now, thanks to you, those stories live on in your imagination. You've learned about the bravery of the gods, the courage of heroes like Sigurd and Beowulf, and the mysteries of the nine worlds. You've heard about the end of one world and the beginning of another. These tales aren't just about ancient myths—they're about the timeless values that the Vikings held dear, values that still matter today.

A Legacy That Lives On

The story of Ragnarok shows us that endings are never truly the end—they are the start of something new. And as long as we remember the lessons of the past, the spirit of the gods, the heroes, and the magical creatures of Norse mythology will live on. Just like the Vikings who told these tales to their children, you too can share these stories, keeping the legends alive for generations to come. Who knows? Maybe one day, you'll be the storyteller by the fire, inspiring others with the incredible tales of the Viking gods and their adventures.

So grab your imaginary shield, young adventurer, and set out on your next quest with the bravery of Odin, the strength of Thor, and the cunning of Loki. The world is full of possibilities, and with the spirit of the Vikings in your heart, you're ready to face whatever comes your way!

Did You Know?

- The word "Ragnarok" comes from Old Norse and means "fate of the gods" or "twilight of the gods."

- Lif and Lifthrasir, the two humans who survived Ragnarok, mean "Life" and "Striving for Life" in Old Norse.

CHAPTER 7:
THE VIKING WAY OF LIFE

◆⬦◉⬦◆

Welcome back, young adventurer! You've learned all about the amazing gods, mighty heroes, and magical creatures of Norse mythology, but have you ever wondered what it would be like to live as a Viking? Vikings didn't spend all their time battling giants or searching for treasure. They also had homes, families, and traditions that made their lives special.

Today, we'll explore what everyday life was like for the Vikings, from their cozy villages to their famous longships. We'll even sit by the fire with them and hear the stories that kept their spirits warm during the long, cold winters. So grab your imaginary shield and let's take a journey back in time to see what it meant to live like a Viking!

Life in a Viking Village: Daily Routines and Traditions

Imagine waking up in a small wooden house with a thatched roof (made out of dried straw or grass), nestled in a village surrounded by rolling hills and thick forests. This is what daily life looked like for many Vikings. Your house would probably be located in a typical Viking village, which would have been made up of small homes called "longhouses." These longhouses were made of wood, stone, or even turf (that's grass and dirt piled up to make thick walls). The longhouses were warm and cozy, with a big fire in the middle to keep everyone warm during the freezing winters.

Vikings lived with their entire family under one roof—parents, children, and sometimes even grandparents. They kept their animals, like sheep, goats, and cows, inside the longhouse too, especially during the winter. Imagine falling asleep every night to the sound of goats bleating and cows mooing!

A typical day in a Viking village started early in the morning. The adults would get up with the sun to milk the cows and feed the animals, while kids helped gather firewood or collect eggs. After a hearty breakfast of porridge or bread, everyone would get to work on their chores.

Viking men often worked as farmers or fishermen. They plowed fields, planted crops like barley and rye, and went fishing in the nearby rivers and seas. When they weren't farming, some of the men would go hunting for deer or wild boar in the forests. Meanwhile, the women spun wool into yarn, wove cloth for clothing, and prepared meals for the family. They also made butter and cheese, which were important parts of the Viking diet.

Even though the Vikings worked hard, they also knew how to have fun! They enjoyed playing games like *hnefatafl* (neh-fah-tah-full), which was a board game that's a bit like chess. Kids would play with wooden toys or practice their skills with a bow and arrow. And whenever there was a special celebration, like a wedding or a successful harvest, the whole village would gather for a feast with music, dancing, and delicious food.

It's true that life in a Viking village wasn't always easy, but it was full of adventure, teamwork, and traditions that brought families and friends together. And best of all, everyone had a part to play, whether it was planting crops, building a house, or just sharing stories by the fire.

Viking Clothing: Dressing for the Elements

Vikings needed to stay warm in their cold northern climate, so they dressed in clothing that was both practical and stylish! They made their clothes from wool, linen, and sometimes animal skins, which helped protect them from the chilly winds and snow. Men typically wore long tunics over trousers, while women put on long dresses with aprons and brooches. Both men and women wore cloaks, which they fastened with decorative pins. Everyone also used sturdy leather shoes or boots to walk through muddy fields and rocky paths.

In the Viking world, clothing wasn't just about staying warm—it was also a way to show off your skill and creativity. Viking women would weave beautiful patterns into the fabrics they wore, and men often added embroidery to their tunics. The richer you were, the fancier your clothes would be. A wealthy Viking might have brightly dyed fabrics and even jewelry made of silver or gold, while a simpler farmer might wear undyed wool in shades of gray or brown. But no matter how wealthy they were, the Vikings were proud of their appearance and took care to dress well!

Viking Religion: Worshiping the Gods

Beyond the importance of dressing for both fashion and function, the Vikings also believed that honoring the gods who watched over them was essential to life. The Vikings believed in the many gods and goddesses we have talked about (and others we haven't even mentioned!), each with their own special powers. They built small shrines in their homes and villages where they could leave offerings, like food or coins, to ask for the gods' protection and blessings.

The most important ceremonies were called *blóts*, which were gatherings where people made offerings to the gods. These ceremonies were especially important during times like harvests or before a big journey. During these ceremonies, the Vikings might sacrifice an animal like a pig or a goat and share a feast in the gods' honor. They believed that by doing this, they could gain the gods' favor which would, in turn, ensure good weather, a successful harvest, or safe travels.

Viking Art and Craftsmanship: Carving, Weaving, and More

Though the Vikings put a lot of faith in the gods, not everything was left up to fate. The Vikings were as talented artistically as they were fierce in battle, which could work to their advantage. They loved to carve intricate designs into wood, stone, and metal, creating beautiful artwork that told stories of their gods, heroes, and adventures. But more importantly, Viking warriors used this talent to decorate their shields and weapons with carvings of dragons and other mythical creatures, which made them look even more fearsome in battle.

But the artistry didn't stop there. Viking women were skilled weavers, creating colorful cloth for clothing and blankets. They used natural dyes made from plants and berries to create shades of red, blue, and yellow. Some of their cloth was so well made that it could last for years, keeping their families warm through many winters.

Vikings also created beautiful jewelry, like rings, brooches, and arm rings, which they wore to show their status and wealth. Some of the most impressive pieces were made of silver and gold, with intricate patterns of knots and animals. Even though they lived in a rough and wild world, the

Vikings had a deep appreciation for beauty and took pride in their craftsmanship.

The Viking Calendar: Celebrating the Seasons

The Vikings were also as in tune with the weather and nature as they were their art, marking the passage of time with festivals that celebrated the changing seasons. These celebrations were a chance for the whole village to come together and give thanks for the harvest or ask the gods for a mild winter. One of the biggest festivals was *Yule*, which was celebrated during the darkest days of winter. Families gathered to feast, tell stories, and light fires to welcome back the sun as the days began to grow longer.

They also celebrated *Ostara*, the spring festival, which was all about new life and growth. It was a time for planting crops and welcoming the warmer weather. In the summer, the Vikings held festivals to honor the sea and the sun, thanking the gods for good fishing and safe voyages.

These festivals were filled with music, dancing, and storytelling. They were a time when the Vikings could forget about their everyday work and enjoy the company of their friends and family. Even though life could be hard, these celebrations reminded the Vikings of the joy and beauty in the world.

Viking Trading: More Than Just Raiders

After discussing the Vikings' eye for beauty and appreciation for the world around them, you could probably guess that while the Vikings are famous for their raids in other lands, they were also skilled traders who traveled far and wide to exchange goods with other cultures. Viking traders sailed to distant lands like the Byzantine Empire, the Caliphate of Baghdad, and even to the rivers of Russia. They traded furs, amber, and walrus ivory from their northern homelands for exotic items like silks, spices, glass beads, and silver coins.

Vikings built trading towns like *Hedeby* and *Birka*, where traders from all over the world would come to exchange goods. These towns were bustling marketplaces where you could hear many different languages spoken and see treasures from lands far beyond the Viking seas.

Trading helped the Vikings learn about new ideas and cultures, and it made them rich enough to build stronger ships and larger homes. The Vikings loved to collect beautiful things, and their trading networks helped them bring a little bit of the world back to their villages.

Viking Ships: How They Traveled the Seas

To travel to these distant places, the Vikings used amazing and well-crafted ships. As they were some of the best sailors in the world, Vikings made ships that were fast, strong, and well-built. These ships were perfect for exploring new lands. Without their ships, the Vikings wouldn't have been able to travel across oceans or reach faraway places like England, Iceland, Greenland, or even North America!

The most famous Viking ship was the longship (also known as longboats). As the name suggests, longships were long and narrow. These boats normally featured a dragon-shaped figurehead carved into the front as well. These dragon heads were meant to scare away sea monsters and enemies! Longships had oars on each side so the crew could row when there wasn't enough wind for the sail. But when the wind was strong, the Vikings raised a large sail that could carry them quickly across the waves.

Longships were perfect for Viking adventures. They were built with flat bottoms, which meant they could sail close to the shore or even up rivers. This allowed the Vikings to explore new lands, trade with other people, and sometimes even raid enemy villages. A Viking crew could travel far and wide, bringing back treasures, new stories, and exotic goods like spices, silver, and silk.

For longer journeys, the Vikings used larger ships called *knarrs*. Knarrs were like the cargo ships of the Viking Age. They could carry food, animals, tools, and other supplies needed for long trips. These ships helped the Vikings settle in new lands, bringing everything they needed to start a new life.

The Vikings had no maps or compasses, but they used the stars, the sun, and even the flight of birds to find their way across the ocean. They knew how to read the winds and the waves, and they believed that the gods, especially Thor, would protect them on their journeys. The Vikings' skill with ships and sailing is one of the reasons they became such great explorers, discovering new lands and creating legends that are still told today!

Viking Warriors and the Code of Honor

If you think about the Vikings, along with their sailing capabilities, you probably also imagine fierce warriors with swords, shields, and helmets. And you're right—Vikings were known for their bravery in battle. But, being a Viking warrior wasn't just about fighting; it was also about following a special code of honor.

The Vikings believed that a true warrior was someone who was brave, strong, and loyal to their family and friends. They thought that facing danger with courage was the most honorable thing a person could do. This idea of honor was so important to them that they had a special word for it: *drengskapr*, which means "the spirit of a true warrior."

When Viking warriors went into battle, they carried round wooden shields and wore helmets to protect themselves. They fought with swords, axes, and spears. Some warriors even carried "long axes," which were huge battle axes with long handles that could cut through enemy shields. Viking warriors trained from a young age, learning how to fight with skill and speed.

One of the most famous types of Viking warriors was the *berserker*. Berserkers were fierce fighters who went into battle wearing animal skins, like bears or wolves. They believed that the spirit of the animal would make them stronger and fiercer in battle. When a berserker charged into a fight, it was said that nothing could stop them!

But the Vikings also believed in fairness and respect for their enemies. If two warriors wanted to settle a disagreement, they might challenge each other to a *holmgang*, a type of duel where the winner would prove their honor. They fought bravely, but also made sure to follow the rules. Thus, it was rare that people cheated or fought unfairly.

The Viking code of honor wasn't just for warriors—it was something that everyone in the village respected. It meant standing up for what was right, protecting your family, and always keeping your promises. The Vikings believed that if you lived with honor, the gods would notice and welcome you to Valhalla after you died to join Odin's feast and celebrate your courage forever!

The Importance of Storytelling Around the Fire

After a long day of farming, fishing, battling, or sailing, the Vikings loved to gather around the fire in their longhouses. As the flames crackled and the shadows danced on the walls, they shared stories of gods, heroes, and faraway lands. These stories were called *sagas*, and they were a very important part of Viking life.

Vikings didn't have books or TVs, so they entertained each other with their voices and their imagination. The village *skald* (a type of poet) would often lead the storytelling. Skalds were like the rock stars of the Viking Age—they memorized long poems or legends and brought them to life through words alone. Everyone would listen closely as the skald told the tale of Beowulf's battle with Grendel, or Thor's fight with the World Serpent.

But storytelling wasn't just about entertainment—it was also a way to pass down important lessons and teach the younger generation about their ancestors. By telling these stories, the Vikings taught their children how to be brave like Thor, wise like Odin, and clever like Loki. Young Vikings learned about the strength of their ancestors and the power of their gods, which made them feel connected to the world around them.

One of the most popular sagas was the *Prose Edda*, a collection of tales about the gods and the creation of the world. This collection recounted how Odin created the first humans from two trees, how Loki's tricks caused trouble, and how the gods fought to protect the world from giants. Each story had a lesson, reminding the Vikings of the values that mattered most—courage, loyalty, and the importance of friendship.

Storytelling was also a way to keep the Viking spirit alive during the long, dark winters, when the days were short and the nights seemed endless. As the wind howled outside and snow covered the ground, the warmth of the fire and the magic of the stories made everything feel cozy and safe.

Even today, the stories that the Vikings told around their fires continue to inspire people all over the world. They remind us that a great story can light up even the darkest night, and that the adventures of our heroes live on as long as we keep telling their tales.

A Day in the Life of a Viking

Now, it's time for you to put yourself in the shoes of a Viking and imagine how a day in your life might look. You would probably wake up in your cozy longhouse, help your parents feed the animals, and then head out to the fields or the sea to do your work. In the afternoon, you might practice with your wooden sword, dreaming of becoming a warrior. As the sun sets, you would surely gather around the fire with your family, listening to stories of gods and heroes, and thinking about the great adventures that await you.

Remember, you don't need to battle giants or sail across the ocean to live like a Viking. All you need is a bit of bravery, a sense of adventure, and a love for the stories that make life magical.

Finding the Viking Spirit Within You

So remember, young adventurer, that no matter what challenges you face, there is always a chance for a new beginning, just like in the stories of the Vikings. Maybe your challenges won't be as big as fighting giants or facing down a world-ending dragon, but that doesn't make them any less important. Like the gods who stood their ground during Ragnarok, you too can find the courage to face whatever comes your way. Whether it's trying something new, standing up for a friend, or simply facing a tough day, the Viking spirit is inside you, urging you to be brave.

And just as the world of the Vikings was filled with wonder and adventure, so too is our world. There are still mysteries to explore, stories to tell, and adventures to embark on. The Vikings believed that courage, resilience, and the hope for a better future could make even the toughest challenges worthwhile. And now that you know their stories, you can carry that same belief with you, no matter where your own journey takes you.

Did You Know?

- Viking longships were so well-built that modern archaeologists have found Viking shipwrecks that are still in good condition after over 1,000 years!

- The word "berserk" comes from the Viking *berserkers*, who were known for their wild and fearless fighting style.

- Vikings loved eating *skyr*, a thick, yogurt-like food that is still popular in Iceland today!

- Now that you know all about the Viking way of life, you're ready to explore even more of their amazing world. Are you excited to hear more stories about brave heroes and legendary battles? Let's keep turning the pages and continue our Viking adventure together!

CONCLUSION: YOUR OWN VIKING JOURNEY

Though this might be the end of our journey through the world of Viking legends and Norse mythology, it isn't the end of the story. In many ways, it's just the beginning. You've learned about brave gods, magical creatures, and epic battles. Now it's time to think about what these stories mean for us today and how you can continue your own Viking adventure. So sit back, grab your imaginary horn of mead (or juice!), and let's explore the lessons and magic that the Viking myths have left for us.

Norse Myths and Lessons for Today

You might be wondering, "Why are stories about gods and giants from so long ago still important?" Well, the answer is simple: remember that Norse myths aren't just old tales—they're filled with lessons that can help us understand our world today. Even though we don't ride in longships or battle sea serpents anymore, the spirit of the Viking stories can still teach us how to live with bravery, kindness, and curiosity.

Think about Thor, who never gave up when facing the giants of Jotunheim. Or Loki, who learned that even the cleverest tricks have consequences. And what about Freya and her love for nature, or Odin and his endless search for wisdom? Each of these characters faced challenges, just like we do, and they learned important lessons along the way.

Lessons from the Stories: Courage, Friendship, and Honesty

The stories of the Vikings are full of heroes, but you don't need a magical hammer or a talking horse to be a hero. The myths teach us that courage, friendship, and honesty are the true qualities of a hero, and these are things that anyone can have!

- **Courage**: Like Thor, you can show courage by facing your fears, whether it's trying something new or standing up for a friend. Courage doesn't mean you're never afraid; it means you keep going even when you are.

- **Friendship**: Even when the Viking gods disagreed, they knew the value of friendship. Loki and Thor might have been opposites, but they went on many adventures together and helped each other out. Friendship means being there for each other, even when things get tough.

- **Honesty**: Odin valued wisdom and truth, and he taught the Vikings that being honest and true to yourself is one of the greatest strengths. Telling the truth, keeping promises, and being fair were all important in the Viking world, just as they are today.

These lessons from the Viking sagas can help us in our own lives. Whether you're at school, with your family, or exploring new things, remember the values that made the Viking heroes great!

How the Myths Explain Nature: Thunderstorms, Rainbows, and More

One of the coolest things about Norse mythology is how it explains the wonders of nature. Before science, the Vikings used these stories to make sense of the world around them. Even though we now know why lightning strikes and how rainbows are made, the old myths give us a magical way of seeing these things.

- **Thunderstorms**: Have you ever heard thunder rumbling in the sky? The Vikings believed that it was Thor riding his chariot across the clouds. While he rode, he swung Mjolnir, which created thunder as he went.

So the next time you hear a thunderstorm, you can imagine Thor up there, battling giants!

- **Rainbows**: Rainbows were more than just pretty colors to the Vikings—they were parts of the Bifrost (the magical bridge that connected Asgard and Midgard) peaking through. They believed that every time a rainbow appeared, it meant that a god might be traveling between worlds.

- **The Northern Lights**: If you're lucky enough to see the beautiful Northern Lights dancing in the sky, you're looking at something that the Vikings believed were reflections of the Valkyries' armor as they rode across the sky. These colorful lights made the cold nights of the north feel even more magical.

These stories remind us that the world is full of wonder and mystery, and that there's always room for a little magic in our lives, even when we know the science behind it.

Why the Vikings' Beliefs Still Inspire Us Today

So, why do the Viking stories still inspire people all around the world, even after more than a thousand years? It's because these stories remind us of the things that are most important—like bravery, love, adventure, and never giving up. They show us that even the strongest heroes have flaws, and that even the trickiest situations can be solved with a little bit of cleverness.

The Vikings' belief in a world full of gods, giants, and hidden realms helps us see that life can be an adventure, too. It encourages us to explore new places, learn new things, and find our own paths, just like the Viking explorers did. Whether you dream of sailing across the sea, discovering new lands, or simply making a new friend, the spirit of the Vikings lives on in every act of bravery and curiosity.

How to Explore More Viking Stories

Your adventure doesn't have to end with this book! There are lots of ways to keep exploring the world of Viking legends and learn even more about the gods, heroes, and magical creatures you've met.

- **Read More Books**: Look for books about Norse mythology at your library. You can find books that tell more stories about the gods, or even real-life tales about Viking explorers and their journeys.

- **Watch Viking Shows and Movies**: There are lots of movies and TV shows inspired by Norse mythology and Viking adventures. Just make sure to check with an adult to find something that's right for you!

- **Visit Museums**: If you live near a museum with a Viking exhibit, you can see real Viking artifacts like swords, shields, and even pieces of longships! It's a great way to see how the Vikings lived and imagine what life was like in a Viking village.

- **Explore Online**: There are websites and virtual museum tours that let you explore Viking history from your computer. You can even find videos that teach you how to write in *runes*, the ancient Viking alphabet!

By exploring these resources, you'll become a true Viking expert, ready to share your knowledge with friends and family!

Final Words of Wisdom from the Viking Sagas

Before we say goodbye, let's remember some of the best lessons from the Viking sagas:

- **Be brave, like Thor, even when things seem impossible.**

- **Be wise, like Odin, always searching for knowledge.**

- **Be clever, like Loki, but remember to use your skills for good.**

- **And above all, be kind and true, like the heroes of old, who valued friendship and honor.**

These stories have been passed down for generations, and now you are part of their journey. By learning about the Viking myths, you now have the power to keep these tales alive for the next generation of adventurers.

GLOSSARY OF VIKING TERMS

—————✦◇◇◉◇◇✦—————

Welcome to the Glossary of Viking Terms! Here, you'll find definitions for some of the trickiest words and names from Norse mythology. As these words come from Old Norse, the language of the Vikings, they might seem a bit strange at first. But don't worry! With this guide, you'll become a master of Viking vocabulary in no time. We've also included a pronunciation guide to help you sound like a true Norse storyteller!

Aesir (AY-seer)

- **Definition**: The main group of gods in Norse mythology, who live in Asgard. They include Odin, Thor, Freya, and others. They are often at war with the Jotnar (giants).

- **Example**: Odin is the leader of the Aesir, the gods who protect Asgard from the giants of Jotunheim.

Asgard (AZ-gard)

- **Definition**: The home of the Aesir gods, high above the clouds. It is connected to the human world, Midgard, by the rainbow bridge, Bifrost.

- **Example**: Asgard is where Thor and Odin live and where brave warriors go after they die in battle.

Bifrost (BEE-frost)

- **Definition**: The rainbow bridge that connects Asgard, the realm of the gods, with Midgard, the world of humans.

- **Example**: The god Heimdall guards Bifrost, making sure no enemies cross into Asgard.

Fenrir (FEN-reer)

- **Definition**: A giant wolf and the son of Loki. Fenrir is prophesied to bring great danger to the gods during Ragnarok.

- **Example**: The gods tried to bind Fenrir with chains, but he will break free during Ragnarok.

Freya (FRAY-uh)

- **Definition**: The goddess of love, beauty, and war. Freya is a member of the family of the Vanir gods, but she lives in Asgard. She rides a chariot pulled by two giant cats.

- **Example**: Freya is known for her magical necklace, *Brísingamen*, which shines like the stars.

Heimdall (HIME-dahl)

- **Definition**: The watchman of Asgard who guards the rainbow bridge, Bifrost. He has incredible sight and hearing.

- **Example**: Heimdall can hear grass growing and the footsteps of a person hundreds of miles away!

Jotun (YO-tun)

- **Definition**: Another word for a giant. Jotnar (plural of Jotun) are often enemies of the Aesir gods and live in Jotunheim.

- **Example**: Thor often travels to Jotunheim to battle the Jotnar.

Jotunheim (YO-tun-hime)

- **Definition**: The realm of the giants, or Jotnar. It is one of the Nine Worlds connected by Yggdrasil.

- **Example**: Jotunheim is cold and wild, filled with towering mountains and fierce giants.

Loki (LOH-kee)

- **Definition**: A trickster god known for causing trouble, but also for helping the gods in tricky situations. He can change his shape and is the father of many monsters.

- **Example**: Loki's tricks often get him into trouble with the other gods, especially Thor.

Midgard (MID-gard)

- **Definition**: The world where humans live, surrounded by an ocean that is home to the World Serpent, *Jormungandr*.

- **Example**: Midgard is connected to Asgard by the rainbow bridge, Bifrost.

Mjolnir (MYOL-neer)

- **Definition**: Thor's magical hammer, which creates thunder and lightning. It is powerful enough to defeat giants and always returns to Thor's hand.

- **Example**: Mjolnir is one of the most powerful weapons in Norse mythology.

Niflheim (NIF-el-hime)

- **Definition**: Niflheim is a cold, misty world full of ice and darkness. It is also one of the Nine Realms. It existed before all other worlds, along with *Muspelheim*.
- **Example**: Niflheim is home to freezing rivers and icy mists.

Odin (OH-din)

- **Definition**: The king of the gods and ruler of Asgard. Odin is the god of wisdom, war, and poetry. He sacrificed an eye for wisdom.
- **Example**: Odin rides his eight-legged horse, *Sleipnir*, and is often seen with his two ravens, *Huginn* and *Muninn*.

Ragnarok (RAHG-nuh-rahk)

- **Definition**: The end of the world in Norse mythology, when a great battle will take place between the gods and the giants. It is foretold that this battle will lead to the death of many gods and the rebirth of the world.

- **Example**: During Ragnarok, Thor must battle the World Serpent, Jormungandr, and Odin must face Fenrir, the giant wolf.

Sleipnir (SLAYP-neer)

- **Definition**: This is Odin's magical eight-legged horse, known for being the fastest in the Nine Worlds.

- **Example**: Sleipnir can carry Odin across the sky and between the different realms in no time.

Surtr (SOOR-tur)

- **Definition**: A giant with a flaming sword who will lead the fire giants in the battle of Ragnarok. He is destined to set the world on fire.

- **Example**: Surtr's sword burns so brightly that it will light up the sky during Ragnarok.

Thor (THOR)

- **Definition**: The god of thunder and lightning, known for his strength and his hammer, Mjolnir. He is the protector of Midgard.

- **Example**: Thor is the son of Odin and often travels to Jotunheim to fight giants.

Valhalla (Val-HALL-uh)

- **Definition**: Odin's great hall in Asgard, where brave warriors go after they die in battle. In Valhalla, they train for war and feast until the end of the world.

- **Example**: The Valkyries carry fallen warriors to Valhalla, where they prepare for the final battle of Ragnarok.

Valkyries (VAL-keer-eez)

- **Definition**: Warrior maidens who serve Odin. They choose which warriors will go to Valhalla after dying in battle.

- **Example**: The Valkyries ride across the sky on winged horses, carrying brave souls to Valhalla.

Vanaheim (VAH-nuh-hime)

- **Definition**: The home of the Vanir, the group gods associated with nature and fertility. They live in harmony with the Aesir after making peace.

- **Example**: Freya and Frey are two of the Vanir gods who moved to Asgard.

Yggdrasil (IG-druh-sil)

- **Definition**: The World Tree that connects all nine worlds in Norse mythology. Its roots and branches reach into every realm.

- **Example**: Yggdrasil holds up the universe. Creatures like the giant eagle and the dragon, *Nidhogg,* live among its branches and roots.

Jormungandr (YOUR-mun-gand)

- **Definition**: The World Serpent, a giant snake that wraps around Midgard. He is one of Loki's children and an enemy of Thor.

- **Example**: Jormungandr is so large that he can encircle the entire world and bite his own tail.

And there you have it, brave reader—a glossary of the most important words and names in Norse mythology! Use this guide to help you understand the stories, or impress your friends with your knowledge of Viking words. Happy adventuring, and may the spirit of the Viking sagas stay with you wherever your journey takes you!

BONUS SECTION:
THE VIKING ACTIVITY CORNER

✦ ◇◈◇ ✦

Welcome, creative adventurer, to the Viking Activity Corner! Here, you'll find fun projects that let you use your imagination and hands to bring the world of the Vikings to life. Whether you want to make your own magical rune stones, draw and color Viking gods, or write your own epic saga, this section is all about having fun and creating something special. Time to unleash your inner Viking!

Create Your Own Viking Rune Stones

Did you know that the Vikings used a special alphabet called *runes*? Runes were carved into stones, wood, and metal. The Vikings used this alphabet to write messages, mark graves, and create magical symbols for protection and good luck. Now, you can make your own Viking rune stones at home!

What You'll Need:

- Small, flat stones (you can find these outside or buy them at a craft store)
- A permanent marker or paint pen
- A guide to the runic alphabet (you can find one online or at the library)
- Optional: Acrylic sealant to protect your designs

Instructions:

1. **Clean Your Stones**: If you found your stones outside, give them a quick wash and let them dry. Clean stones are easier to draw on!

2. **Pick Your Runes**: Use your guide to the runic alphabet to pick a few runes that mean something special to you. Runes can represent letters, but some also have meanings like "strength," "friendship," or "courage."

3. **Draw the Runes**: Use your marker or paint pen to carefully draw one rune on each stone. Make sure to take your time so the runes come out nice and clear!

4. **Let Them Dry**: If you're using paint, let your stones dry completely before touching

them. If you want to keep your rune stones outside, you can spray them with acrylic sealant to protect them from the weather.

5. **Create Your Own Meanings**: Write down what each rune means to you, or create a special story about how you found your magical rune stones.

Ideas for Using Your Rune Stones:

- Use them as lucky charms to keep in your pocket.

- Create a small pouch to keep your runes and draw one each day for inspiration.

- Give them to friends as gifts with a special message!

Now you have your very own set of Viking rune stones, just like the ones the ancient Norse used to make! What will your runes say?

Draw and Color Viking Gods and Creatures

Do you have a favorite Viking god, like Thor with his mighty hammer, or a beloved magical creature, like the World Serpent? Now's your chance to bring them to life with your drawing skills! This activity will help you imagine what these incredible characters might look like.

What You'll Need:

- Drawing paper
- Pencils, crayons, colored pencils, or markers
- A guide or pictures of Norse gods and creatures for inspiration

Instructions:

1. **Choose a Character**: Pick a Viking god, hero, or creature that you'd like to draw. It could be Thor, Loki, Odin, or even a creature like Fenrir the wolf or Sleipnir the eight-legged horse.

2. **Sketch Your Drawing**: Use a pencil to sketch the outline of your character. Don't worry if it's not perfect—drawing is all about having fun and using your imagination!

3. **Add Details**: Think about what makes your character special. Is Thor holding Mjolnir in his hand? Does Loki have a mischievous grin? Add details to make your character unique.

4. **Color It In**: Once you're happy with your sketch, use crayons, colored pencils, or markers to color your drawing. Be creative

with your colors—after all, no one knows exactly what the Viking gods looked like!

5. **Give Your Drawing a Name**: Write the name of your character at the bottom of the drawing, and maybe even add a short description or a fun fact about them.

Ideas for Your Viking Art:

- Draw a scene of Thor battling Jormungandr, the World Serpent.

- Create a portrait of Freya riding her chariot pulled by giant cats.

- Imagine what the Viking village of Asgard might look like and draw the gods gathered together.

Hang your drawings on the wall to create your own Viking art gallery, or share them with friends and family! Your art can help keep the stories of the Viking gods alive.

Write Your Own Viking Saga

Do you like telling stories? How about writing your own Viking saga, just like the ancient storytellers used to do? A saga is a long story filled with great adventures, brave heroes, and magical events. Now, it's your turn to become a Viking storyteller!

What You'll Need:

- A notebook or paper
- A pencil or pen
- Your imagination!

Instructions:

1. **Choose a Hero**: Think about who you want your story to be about. Will your hero be a Viking warrior, a brave explorer, or maybe even a clever trickster like Loki?

2. **Pick an Adventure**: What will your hero do? Will they sail across the sea in search of new lands, battle a dangerous sea monster, or search for a hidden treasure? Use your imagination to come up with an exciting quest!

3. **Create a Setting**: Where does your story take place? Maybe it's in a Viking village by the sea, deep in the snowy forests, or in a magical land like Asgard or Jotunheim.

4. **Add a Challenge**: Every great Viking saga has a challenge or a problem to solve. Maybe your hero has to defeat a giant, outsmart a tricky creature, or find a way to cross a stormy sea. What obstacles will your hero face?

5. **Write the Ending**: How does your story end? Does your hero succeed in their quest, or do they learn an important lesson along the way? Think about how you want to wrap up your saga.

Story Starter Ideas:

- "Once upon a time, a young Viking named Astrid set out on a longship to find the legendary island of gold, but she soon discovered she was not alone on the sea…"

- "In the land of ice and snow, Thor faced his greatest challenge yet when a powerful giant challenged him to a duel…"

- "Loki had stolen the golden apples of Asgard, and it was up to a young warrior named Erik to track him down before the gods lost their strength forever…"

Share Your Saga:

- Read your story aloud to your family, just like a Viking *skald* would.

- Illustrate scenes from your saga and create a picture book.

- Write new chapters whenever you think of new adventures for your hero!

With these fun activities, you can continue exploring the world of the Vikings long after you finish reading this book. Who knows? Maybe you'll discover a hidden talent for drawing, writing, or even rune-crafting!

Remember, being a Viking isn't just about battles and bravery. It's about using your imagination, being curious about the world, and finding a new adventure every day. So, grab your pencil, pick up a stone, and let your creativity take you on your own Viking journey!

Did You Have Fun?

We hope you enjoyed the Viking Activity Corner and learned something new along the way. And remember—your Viking adventures are just beginning. As long as you keep exploring, learning, and sharing stories, the spirit of the Vikings will always be with you!

Happy adventuring, young Viking!

REFERENCES

———✦◇◇◉◇◇✦———

This book was compiled using resources from the following:

- "Children of Ash and Elm: A History of the Vikings" by Neil Price
- "The Complete Illustrated Guide to Viking Mythology" by John Haywood
- "Myths and Symbols in Pagan Europe: Early Scandinavian and Celtic Religions" by H.R. Ellis Davidson
- "Myths of the Norsemen: From the Eddas and Sagas" by H.A. Guerber
- "Norse Mythology" by Neil Gaiman
- "The Norse Myths" by Kevin Crossley-Holland
- "The Prose Edda" by Snorri Sturluson
- "The Sagas of the Icelanders"
- "Viking Age: Everyday Life During the Extraordinary Era of the Norsemen" by Kirsten Wolf

- "Viking Myths & Sagas: Retold from Ancient Norse Texts" by Rosalind Kerven
- "Vikings: Life and Legend" by Gareth Williams and Peter Pentz
- National Museum of Denmark: Vikings (natmus.dk)
- The British Museum's Viking Collection (britishmuseum.org)
- The Icelandic Saga Database (sagadb.org)
- The Viking Society for Northern Research (viking-society.org)
- The World History Encyclopedia (world history.org)

These resources provided valuable insights into Norse mythology, Viking history, and the culture that shaped the stories in this book.

FREE BONUS FROM HBA: EBOOK BUNDLE

Greetings!

First, thank you for reading our books.

Now, we invite you to join our VIP list. As a welcome gift we offer the History & Mythology eBook Bundle below for free. Plus, you can be the first to receive new books and exclusives! Remember it's 100% free to join.

Simply click the link below to join.

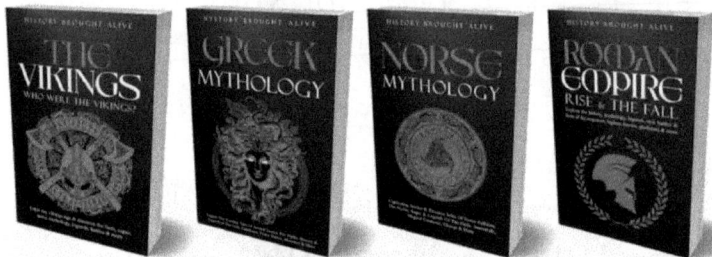

FREE DOWNLOAD

https://www.subscribepage.com/hba

Keep up to date with us on:

YouTube: History Brought Alive

Facebook: History Brought Alive

www.historybroughtalive.com

Check out the other books in this series

- African Legends For Kids: Kings, Queens, Heroes, Spirits, Myths, Tales & More From Africa

- Aztec Legends For Kids: Gods, Warriors, Myths, Wonders & More From Ancient Mexico

- Celtic Legends For Kids: Heroes, Fairies, Warriors, Myths, Magic & More From The Ancient Celts

- Chinese Legends For Kids: Emperors, Dragons, Gods, Heroes, Myths & More From Ancient China

- English Legends For Kids: Knights, Castles, Kings, Queens, Myths & More From Old England

- Incan Legends For Kids: Emperors, Warriors, Myths, Treasures & More From Ancient Peru

- Indian Legends For Kids: Gods, Goddesses, Warriors, Sages, Myths, Epics & More From Ancient India

- Irish Legends For Kids: Heroes, Druids, Myths, Magic & More From Ancient Ireland

- Japanese Legends For Kids: Samurai, Spirits, Emperors, Myths, Magic & More From Japan

- Mesopotamian Legends For Kids: Kings, Queens, Gods, Myths, Wonders & More From The Cradle Of Civilization

- Native American Legends For Kids: Spirits, Chiefs, Warriors, Myths, Sacred Tales & More

- Persian Legends For Kids: Heroes, Kings, Myths, Epics & More From Ancient Persia

- Russian Legends For Kids: Czars, Fairies, Warriors, Folktales, Myths & More From Russia

- Scottish Legends For Kids: Warriors, Fairies, Kings, Queens, Myths, Legends & More From Scotland

- Thai Legends For Kids: Kings, Queens, Demons, Heroes, Myths, Sacred Tales & More From Thailand

- Viking & Norse Legends For Kids: Gods, Warriors, Myths, Heroes & More From The From The Ancient Norse World

- Welsh Legends For Kids: Dragons, Heroes, Prophecies, Myths, Magic & More From Ancient Wales

and follow us on
www.historybroughtalive.com and
https://www.youtube.com/@historybroughtalive